Saved Twice

Andy Peterson

with Donald James Parker

1 Peter 5:8-9
Be self-controlled and alert.
Your enemy the devil prowls around life a
roaring lion looking for someone to devour.
Resist him, standing firm in the faith.

ISBN 13: 978-1-9392191-7-6

Published by Sword of the Spirit Publishing

www.swordofspirit.net

MOUNTAIN LION STATISTICS

- The American lion's scientific name is *Puma (Felis) concolor,* and sometimes referred to as "the cat of many names." Known as Cougars, Pumas, Panthers and Mountain Lions.
- Territory can range 10-350 square miles.
- 130 degree binocular vision. 287 degree total vision. Night vision is 6 times better at night then humans.
- Tries to eat 8-10 lbs. of meat per day to survive.
- They surprise attack to sever the spine or bust the vertebrae until their kill stops breathing.
- Their protractile sharp claws do not show marks in their tracks.
- Males can weight 175 lbs. Females 125 lbs. Some known to exceed 200 lbs.
- Males can measure 8 feet in length nose to tail. Females 5 to 7 feet.
- Eat 100% meat they prefer to kill to ensure it is fresh.
- Carry 100 lbs. in its mouth in a sprint the length of a football field (100 yards).
- Able to take down an elk, deer, porcupine, coyote and even moose (favorite is deer).
- They can jump 40 feet horizontal in length.
- Leap over a 15 foot high fence.
- Leap over an 8 foot high fence with a 100 lb. deer in its mouth.
- Travel many miles at 10 mph.
- Reach speeds of 50 mph in a sprint.

- If you encounter a mountain lion, STOP. DO NOT RUN. Maintain eye contact. Stand tall. Look bigger by opening your coat or raising your arms. Slowly wave your arms and speak firmly. Throw items at the lion if necessary. Give the cat room and time to move on. In the rare event of an attack, fight back. GO FOR THE EYES. Most people succeed in driving the mountain lion away.

Revelation 5:5
Do not weep! See, the Lion of the tribe of Judah, the Root of David, has triumphed. He is able to open the scroll and its seven seals.

DEDICATION

Cortney, your unconditional love and prayers you have shown me over the many years are remarkable! Thank you for your countless hours and patience, taking my crazy thinking, and putting them into words on paper for others to understand. You continue to stand by my side each and every day in God's presence. You held my hand and set by example how to fully lean on God. For that alone I thank you. Having you as my best friend and wife is truly an honor and I'm so very thankful our amazing Lord allowed me to be a part of your life. You are an amazing and beautiful woman one whom I fall in love with more so each day. I love you!

Riley & Jaden, how exciting and fulfilling it is to watch you grow up (way too fast), be saved and baptized, and run after Jesus! There is nothing more rewarding for a parent when their children open their hearts and live for Christ! Your hugs, kisses and smiles make every day precious. The joy you have brought to my life I will always hold dear. You've made me one happy Daddy! Thank you! I love you both so very much!

Dad, I thank you for the courage you had to drop your pride and shake your comfort zone to share your best friend, Lord and Savior Jesus with me! Without pausing and witnessing to me, none of this would take place.

To the rest of my family, pastors and friends for their never ending love, prayers and support along the way. I am truly grateful for each and every one that helped mold and guide me on my unusual and fascinating journey.

Donald James Parker, after fifteen years and four word smiths later, you've been able to show wonderful

patience with me while putting this story into reality.
Thank you my friend!

John Bristow, thank you so much for the striking and
powerful cover design that will grab thousands to
hopefully change hearts and lives bringing them closer
to the Lord.

Most importantly, thank you Lord for loving me enough
to allow your Son and my Savior, Jesus Christ, to shed
that one drop of blood so that I may be saved…twice!

John 15:13
Greater love has no one than this, than to lay down
one's life for his friends.

CONTENTS

Chapter 1

The Roaring Lion

I drove my vehicle into the almost deserted parking lot at Roxborough State Park twenty-five miles south of Denver. This was my personal playground, meditation getaway, and exercise venue at least once a week when possible. The warm and bright spring sun was high in the sky as I swung my car door open and emerged into the eighty degree heat.

It was noon on April thirtieth of 1998, and the spring flowers were already out in force. I was pumped to get on my trail and begin my ascent up the mountain and my chance to escape from the busy world. Before proceeding to the trail, I stopped by the visitors' center to sign the climbers' registry. I knew the importance of the rangers knowing who was on the mountain in case of any problems.

A park ranger manned the center. I smiled at the familiar face as I inked my signature.

"Hey, what's going on?"

"Not much. Working a little. Have fun on your hike, Andy."

"I plan to. Thanks."

I waved goodbye and wandered over to the bulletin board and scanned it for any notices that might be relevant to my climb. There were new animal sightings listed on the white dry erase board. A reporting of a black bear with two cubs as well as a fox had been posted on the board the week before. The fox hadn't concerned me. A mother bear with cubs would be something I'd be careful to avoid. So I'd need to be a little more cautious during my hike today. I had to laugh at the thought that back in Minnesota, on a typical day, the sightings concentrated on walleyes, wolves, and mosquitoes.

One listing, which had been on the board for about a year, warned people that a mountain lion had been spotted in the vicinity. For some reason that one caught my attention today, even though I had seen it many times. I'd once found the tracks of a mountain lion in the snow, but had never seen an actual cougar in the wild despite my work outside. *Maybe I'll see something cool today like an eagle, black bear, or mountain lion.*

A ranger myself, I worked at Chatfield State Park nearby. Although I worked outside among the wonders of Mother Nature, I never grew tired of the marvels of the world around me. The park I worked in was extremely busy and not a good place to escape from the world. I had discovered this hiking paradise which allowed me to find the seclusion I craved.

I wasted no more time dwelling on the possible wildlife I may potentially see on my three and two tenths mile hike to the summit. After having made sure my boots were laced tightly, I started up Carpenter's Peak Trail, which featured a thousand foot elevation gain and a forty-five degree incline. When I reached the top, I'd be breathing in the thin mountain air 7160 feet above sea level. It wasn't a course designed for couch potatoes. That was part of the appeal of this particular course. I wanted to be totally alone, and I found very little competition for this terrain.

I passed a man toward the bottom of the trail and blew right by him with a less than genuine hello. A short time later, I passed four ladies. Again I paid them superficial attention, inwardly complaining for them blocking my path and making me go around them. It didn't dawn on me at the time, but I just considered them hindrances that I had to go around and not really human beings worthy of my respect. I had no clue how that attitude would shame me later on.

After making the uneventful hike up the steep trail to the peak and working up a sizable sweat, I took a break. I pulled out my trusty water bottle and an orange from the small pack around my waist. A slab of rock invited me to take a load off my feet. I consumed the orange and swallowed half of the contents of the water bottle as I sat there studying the trail and surrounding landscape. The trail, which provided the only way up and down again due to the dense growth of vegetation, was only a foot or two wide at that point.

While resting at the peak, I enjoyed the luxury of studying the tranquil panoramic sights, which never failed to move me. I could actually see Denver International Airport from this point, despite the sixty mile driving distance. I loved to gaze outward from this elevation and feel free. Today, however, I realized I had lots of errands to complete. My stay at the top had to be cut short. I pulled off my shirt, wrapped it around my waist, and began the return trip descent.

Ahead of me down on the trail, two purple and white flowers waved in the breeze, which was increasing in intensity. I glanced around me. Clouds gathered on the horizon as a storm front appeared to be headed my way. Under a ponderosa pine tree a short distance away, I suddenly spotted something brown. *Is that fur? What would a dog be doing up here? Maybe it's a fox? Nah, too big. No way! Oh, my gosh! That's a mountain lion! How cool is this?*

I could feel the rush of excitement bubbling up inside me. I wanted to cry out "look, everyone", but there was no one around to hear me and to share my captivating rare moment of standing before a mountain lion in the wild. As I stood watching the big cat, suddenly the heat of my excitement transformed into the chilliness of fear. Observing a mountain lion from the safety of a car or cage was definitely a cool thing. Being within a few long and powerful strides of this carnivore was becoming less and less attractive by the second.

I realized that this "king of the mountain" predator hadn't noticed me yet. It appeared that the lion had already found something lower on the food chain to munch on. The sound of the cracking of bones within the cavernous mouth of the cougar didn't lessen my mounting terror. Maybe the animal would leave me alone because it already had dinner. But maybe that wouldn't prevent the animal from taking down another weaker creature for future dining.

I remembered that I wasn't totally unarmed. I had a multipurpose, multi-tool army like knife in my pocket. I pulled it out and started opening all the blades so I'd be prepared in case of a sudden charge. As I maneuvered the knife, it dawned on me that the blades would not lock. After deciding that I could potentially injure myself by using it against an attacker, I began to fumble hurriedly to close all but the larger main blade.

My hand slipped as I was trying to close the screwdriver blade. The slight noise emitted sounded as loud as a freight train. I immediately glanced to the spot where the lion had been. Nothing! My blood froze as I calculated that the lion was probably now aware of my presence and perhaps already making a move to stalk me. I didn't have to assume long about that. My eyes darted back and forth, searching. I didn't see him immediately, but then his roaming eyes found their target, crouching on the trail below me, blocking my only escape route.

My eyes locked onto the pair of menacing feline eyes only twenty feet away. I could tell, even at this distance, that the cat's eyes were drilling right into mine. It felt like the animal looked right through me and was reading my mind and feeling my fear. After staring into the cat's eyes for several minutes, I started backing up to let the lion possess the mountain by itself. I hoped the lion would remain planted. However, as soon as the vegetation blocked our vision of one another and ended our game of stare down, the lion leaped and landed right in front of me!

I could see the lines on the whiskered face and four dominant teeth protruding from the snarling mouth. To compound my fear, the attacker emitted loud, deep, vicious snarls which echoed through the canyon. I took one more step backward.

In the blink of an eye, the lion made a move, swatting at me with its lethal paw. I backed up in time to avoid the menacing claws. I then started yelling at the beast and throwing my orange peels from my waist pack at the killer. I also took a swipe of my own with the artificial claw of the death gripped knife I held in my left hand.

The thunderous verbal tirade I unleashed on the cat's ears had no impact upon the predator, but the knife whizzing through the air near its nose seemed to get across the message to the animal that its prey was not totally defenseless nor an easy meal. Being alone right now was suddenly not high on my priority list, but unfortunately there was not a soul around to give me assistance.

The lion took a step uphill and to the right, opening up an opportunity for me to try to work my way down the trail with a backward step. I started to take another step to the rear. Before I could plant my foot again, the cat leaped gashing its razor sharp claws into the left side of my neck forcing both of us a few feet off the trail side by side. With all my might, I jumped up on the trail, just as the lion leaped again narrowly missing my midsection with its razor sharp claws.

I was now in a position to attempt an escape down the trail. Keeping my eyes on the lion and trying not to trip, I backed up just as fast as I could. I knew that a rear attack was exactly what the killer desired, so I was determined not to expose myself to that strategy. The animal effortlessly kept pace with my feverish attempts to backpedal on a trail that was definitely not fashioned for running. In a state of panic, I even used my shirt as a shield to keep the animal away from me, desperately screaming at the powerful animal with every step.

After approximately ninety yards, I arrived at a spot in the trail where three boulders lined up to form steps about three feet down. I stopped just before I reached the boulders and took a hard swing using the waist pack in my right hand. After watching that swing whistle by harmlessly just inches from the cat's face, I followed that up with an even harder second swing using my knife bearing left hand. Again I watched the tip of the knife strike within an inch of the cat's nose. The lion effortlessly moved out of my reach.

The cat stepped back, and I jumped down the boulder-like steps. The stalker quickly positioned itself at the edge of the steps and let loose another blood curdling scream. I now found myself at the same height and at eye level with the ferocious cougar.

When I heard the roar, I swiftly turned to my right and instantly saw the large black throat with the huge white fangs coming at me over the rock cliff. I didn't even have time to blink as the lion, bent on having me as its next meal, charged with the strength of a bull and the speed of a bullet. The lion's throat and fangs contacted me in the face and shoulders, stunning me. I tried my best to react but with little success as both of us hitting the ground with a loud thud.

The weight of the lion combined with the awkwardness of the backward motion of the fall did nothing to shield me from the searing pain of the lion's teeth buried deep within my head. Its upper teeth dug into the back of my skull while the bottom teeth punctured my forehead. The warm, rushing blood seemed to pour from my newly opened wounds. The entire incident was unbelievably shocking with the first massive powerful bite. My neck was locked tightly in the unrelenting grip of its paws; huge, powerful, and choking. The lion's claws tore my flesh apart as if it were paper.

I grunted and strained to try to do anything I could to force the great beast back, but I was under its control. It had me trapped in every imaginable way. The lion's strength was astonishing. My head was caught in its mouth, its front paws tore at my throat, and its back paws were ripping my legs open. I was at the lion's mercy, trapped as both the beast and I tumbled backwards down the hill through the vegetation and down the rocks, snapping off small trees as we rolled.

The lion quickly gained an advantage over me. Because of its quickness, strength and endurance I was no match. I did everything in my power to try to get away from my attacker, but suddenly and brutally the beast's claws dug deeper into my sides and neck. The huge mouth with the four inch killer fangs began to bite down harder on my head.

I was convinced I was at the edge of death and my survival instincts, along with a surge of adrenaline, kicked in and enabled me to hold my own. Our two bodies rolled around for what seemed like an hour. I was more terrified than I had ever been in my entire life. In reality only a few minutes passed.

Our rolling bodies came to a sudden stop slamming into a large brush with a loud thud, but not breaking our mutual hold. The lion was on its back whereas I was up on my hands and knees, directly over the carnivore, whose rear claws dug into each one of my sides. The front claws were digging into each side of my neck with an eerie audible popping sound with each break of the skin. My head was entirely in the lion's mouth with its fangs clamping down into my skull. From the cougar's throat came a deep, gurgling kind of growling, and a sound I had never heard in my brief lifetime. Suddenly I felt its fangs crunch down into my scalp, not once but twice. Hearing the scrape of its fangs against my skull reverberated inside my head.

The prospect and proximity of death horrified me. I wasn't ready to give in to death. I wanted to live, but there was no one around that I could plead to for help, and the odds of defeating the cougar alone were astronomically against me.

It was during this second time of crunching that I began having glimpses of my life's events streaming through my mind. I began to scream. "I don't want to die! Please! I don't want to die!"

But no one heard my voice since I was literally crying out in the wilderness. I started to sob as I began to lose any hope of surviving the ordeal. This fearful moment was as real as I had ever felt in my life thus far. This was definitely not a game. I felt the life being sucked out of me as the threshold of death seemed to be approaching quickly. At that point a high definition movie kicked in right before my eyes, and my life's events paraded through my mind seemingly in slow motion.

Chapter 2

Family Affairs

The movie began as footage from my preschool days before I had started kindergarten. That had been an exciting and fun time for me. Expectations of a future life had been high in my mind. I, along with my friends, had been preparing for the big world, doing things we, up to that time, had only dreamed of doing.

My parents were always talking about doing exciting things in the future and of watching me playing sports and the family traveling together. My dad, always busy, made promises of building things such as a tree house. My folks had made my young life sound like a great big fantasy trip that we would all be making together. I felt as though I was a grown up, ready to tackle the next milestone in life, kindergarten.

My hopes for the realization of the "big happy family dreams" came to a crashing halt. One day I walked past my sister, who was three years older than me. She was sitting on the floor next to the clothes chute on an upper floor of our house.

"What are you doing?" I asked.

"Shhh!" My sister said pointing to the chute.

The voice of our father exited from the door of the chute. "Maybe I'd come home more often if I got the respect I deserved here!"

"Maybe you'd get more respect if you took more responsibility for being a husband and a father!"

I sat down beside my sister and listened to the heated verbal confrontation play out. When the conversation finally culminated after our father beat a hasty exit to his vehicle, I asked, "What's going on?"

My sister shook her head. "I don't know. But it's not good. I don't like it." Thankfully, I had my big sister to lean on during this troubling and confusing period of time.

The memories of sitting by that chute and listening to similar fights after that flowed strongly. The word insecurity was outside my vocabulary at that point, but my young spirit realized that I had begun to feel the effects of it. The comfort of my family and the home I knew was beginning to tumble down. I had felt as though I was all alone, standing out in a field, watching my family as though I was a spectator. And most critically, I felt like I was not being loved by anyone, especially my parents.

My dad spent time at home less and less frequently. He owned a construction company, so it made sense to me when my mother told me that my father was busy at work. But as the fighting became more intense and more frequent, dad seemed to get even busier. I could read in my mother's eyes that she wasn't telling me the whole truth about my father's absences. Both my sister and I knew there was something else going on, but it was beyond our comprehension at such a tender age.

Then the unthinkable happened. Dad officially moved out of the house, causing emotional turmoil to both my mother and us children. And the insecurity I felt increased.

It was at that time that I began believing that I had done something terribly wrong. I suspected that I was the reason our dad moved out, and the thought gnawed at me.

I had been looking forward to becoming a little man and going off to regular school like my older sister and learning all about life. I didn't have to wait until school to receive one lesson that changed my world drastically. The word "divorce" entered my life through the school of hard knocks, leaving a big scar as a result. Most kid's parents in my school were still married as divorce was not as common as it is today.

My sister and I visited our father in his new residence every other weekend. He had originally moved into the office of his business where he slept on a couch and used a hot plate to prepare his meager meals, but now he maintained an apartment downtown, right above the movie theater. One week our father had asked us to sit down at the little square table which occupied the combination kitchen/living room of the small apartment. We normally used that table to play board games as well as eat. We had enjoyed visiting on the weekends because we always did something together as a family. And dad often fixed our favorite meal, homemade spaghetti and peanut butter and jelly sandwiches.

However, on that day we received some news that would change our young lives forever. My sister and I were holding hands while we listened to the words that emerged from the mouth of our father.

"I've told you about my girlfriend, right?" Our father asked.

We nodded.

"She is really fun and pretty and I like her a lot."

"As much as you like us?" I asked.

"No, that will never happen. I like her in a different way. In fact, I want to marry her."

"But what about mom?" My sister asked.

Dad looked us right in the eye. "First of all, I want you to know that you have done nothing that caused your mom and me to break up. I love you both very very much. More than I can even say. I'm afraid your mother and I will never get back together. In fact, we are going to get a divorce."

"Divorce?" I asked.

"That just means that we're going to make our separation official and final. And then I'll be able to marry my girlfriend."

My sister and I sat there in stunned silence.

"The big question that I have for you guys is this. How you would feel about having a couple of new brothers?"

Our eyes got big as he continued.

"My girlfriend has two boys; one of them is your age, Andy, and the other two years older. I would adopt them if you guys were OK with that. It will be your decision if you would want me to marry my girlfriend. If you say absolutely not, then I won't do it."

At first I had weird feelings going through me. I could only classify it as confusion. It was hard for me to hear my father talk about being with a woman other than my mother. *Why would he want to marry someone else?*

"I guess I popped this on you by surprise. I didn't want you finding out from anyone else, and I really want your support and approval. I'm going to go in the kitchen and fix us something to eat and let you kids discuss it and think it over. OK?"

"OK," we echoed in unison without a lot of animation.

I started looking at the bright side of things. Having a couple of new brothers would be kind of fun. In fact, besides having new siblings, we'd get a new second mom, too. Maybe someday, if and when our mother found a new husband, we'd have a new second dad. It would be super around Christmas time and birthday time when I got double presents. I started feeling good about how life was perhaps changing in a positive way. I figured it was time to meet my potential second mom and new brothers.

Chapter 3

Kissing Creature of Kindergarten

My eagerly awaited entrance into kindergarten finally came to pass, but it was not the blockbuster event that I, as a little boy had foreseen. The thrill of going off to school every day couldn't erase the pain of what was happening in my home.

When the news of my father's exodus came down to me, the flood of pent up emotions overwhelmed the dam holding them back. I was mad, sad, and scared, all at the same time. My insecurities in the home and with life began to show up at school. I was really upset and mad, to the point of taking out my feelings on other kids in my class and getting in trouble with my teacher.

For example, every day my kindergarten teacher summoned the students around a piano in the room and conducted music class. During the music lesson and sing-a-long time, the teacher sat at the piano while all of us kids sat behind her listening, singing and learning all about basic music. At least we were supposed to.

As soon as the class was over, it was play time. There was a toy in the room that I fiercely wanted to play with. The problem is that it was popular with other students as well, particularly one boy. The object of our competition was a big wooden semi truck with a trailer.

When the teacher released us from the music lesson and sing-a-long, all of us students would all hurry back to the entertainment table to pick up the toy we wanted to play with. It was pretty clear to me that if I got closer to that table, I'd have a better chance of getting the truck I coveted. When the other students situated themselves for the class, I sat at the very back on the side of the toy table. Unfortunately my rival did the same.

While music class was going on, I got the brilliant idea to slide back a little further from the piano and toward the truck. My competitor did the same. I repeated as did the other boy. The open space between us two boys and the rest of the class was growing. I slid back again just as the teacher turned around.

A voice reverberating and loud, as if spoken through a bullhorn, rang through the classroom. "Andy Peterson! This is not how we behave during music! Come up here and sit next to me."

My face burned with embarrassment as I trudged up to the piano bench and sat right beside her. I looked back at the other boy, who grinned in exultation over the fact that he was sitting much closer to the prize than I and that I had been busted.

The teacher continued with the song she'd been playing as if nothing had happened. There was now no way I would be able to reach the truck first. My anger burned within me, contemplating how unfair it was that the other boy was not forced to move up by the teacher as well.

I hadn't gotten away with my little trick. And once again in life, I was powerless to change an unfair situation. This situation of not being able to control the problem led to a chronic coloring outside the behavioral lines, which made me a problem for those in authority as well as my peers. I didn't let that one defeat discourage me from trying to get what I wanted. My rival and I continued to battle over that truck during the rest of the school year. Sitting next to the teacher, on or near the piano bench, during music class became a regular occurrence, since I usually got caught pushing the limits.

During my kindergarten year, my dad married his girlfriend. The wedding took place in the back yard of my father's parents' country home. There was plenty of room as grandma and grandpa had a huge back yard with a lot of pine trees. I was put to work as me and my brothers-to-be got to help set up the folding chairs and string ribbon for decorations. The eldest of the new brothers was wearing a sling to protect an elbow he had broken at school during recess the day before.

On the day of the wedding our dad told my sister and I that we would be in the wedding, but afterward, at the end of the day, we would have to go back to our mother's house. I wondered why we weren't important enough to be able to stay with our dad on his special day. Didn't he love us anymore or not as much as he did his new wife? My head was spinning with all that was happening, especially the bouncing back and forth between two households and my father moving yet a third time.

One mitigating factor in my behalf that I was too young to understand at the time was that my father married a very loving woman. If my dad had brought more conflict into my life instead of love, I really would have been messed up.

Life was totally out of control from my perspective. I was spending a lot of time with different babysitters and at my grandma's house. Memories of sitting in the corner at school for something I did or said stung me like a small swarm of bees. I had been teased a lot by my classmates after being disciplined, making me even more angry and unsocial.

What had I done wrong or what was I doing wrong? Why did my parents break up our family? Was it because of something I had done? That was a question that I had to find an answer to. Only then would I be able to begin feeling better about myself. But what could I, as a kindergartener, really do to resolve the situation?

Another behavior problem brought me into conflict with both fellow students and teachers. I had a habit of chasing the girls and kissing them during recess. The playground supervisor yelled at me frequently. After I kissed a girl, she often tattled to a teacher, and I found myself being punished yet again. I even earned the nickname of "the kissing creature".

I found a little adventure in my life, in addition to
my smooching activity. One night I'd been permitted to
take a sip of the beer someone was casually drinking.
It was my first encounter with alcohol, but certainly
wouldn't be my last. Another night someone left an
open can of beer on the counter. I emptied it - not into
the sink but into my mouth. My next blatant case of
booze larceny would not occur for three years, but I set
a precedent for my life at an early age.

It seemed like every day was a battle for me.
School wasn't all bad as I got to play with all kinds of
new toys, playground equipment, and other cool new
things. The ripping apart of my family was the biggest
challenge to deal with. While my father had brought
one new woman into my life, my mother had dated a
few guys over the next couple of years putting me into
a position of dealing with men who weren't my father.

My parents used me as a middle man for their
communications. I hated the fact that they could not
have a meaningful conversation with each other but
had to relay information through my sister and I.
Dealing with difficult situations and conflict soon made
me desire to escape to wherever life was easiest.
Sometimes that was with dad and sometimes it was
with mom. Sometimes it was with one grandmother
and her amazing spaghetti with meatballs and other

times with my other grandmother and her grape Kool-Aid and one-of-a-kind oatmeal cookies. As independent as I was, I found it easier to be alone most of the time, walking around the park, neighborhood or town to do whatever I pleased without anyone knowing where I was or what I was up to.

I did find some allies in the kitchen crew at school. They knew I hated hot dogs and when that particular item was on the menu, they would slip me a ham and cheese salad. This was a lesson in how I could apply my charm and my boyish good looks to get what I wanted.

My enlightening year of kindergarten came to an end, but the pain and the problems did not go away.

Chapter 4

Elementary My Dear Andy

First grade brought new challenges. Now I
spent all day in school instead of just a half a day. I
was subjected to more opportunity to misbehave than
had been the case in kindergarten.

My mother lived only a block away from the
front door of the school. One day, after I had walked to
school, I decided I didn't really want to sit in the
classroom that day. I knew my mother would be
teaching all day at another school in a town nearby and
wouldn't be home until that afternoon. My sister was in

school as well. The house with the locked front door was only one block away from me, and it was empty. And I just happened to have a spare key. The only thing between me, freedom from the classroom and a rendezvous with the television set was a nagging reminder that I didn't want more trouble. After weighing the odds, I decided I could get away with it. I retraced my steps to the house and let myself in. Silence was golden. However, I soon shattered the silence by flicking on the television. Settling down on the couch with some junk food to watch whatever channel I desired seemed like a slice of paradise. My first taste into the world of skipping school went by without incident. I made sure that I left the house before my mother returned at 3:30 p.m. from her teaching job. I found that I could monitor the house from a nearby park to know when she returned. It became evident to me that I also could track her departures from the same spot.

My success emboldened me to begin planning my absences in advance. On the days I decided to stay home, I would walk out of the house carrying my backpack and head down the sidewalk toward the city park adjacent to my elementary school. When I got halfway through the park, I would hide behind some trees near a rock formation and a city water tower, watching and waiting for my mother to leave the house for her job in a nearby city ten miles away. As soon as she left, I would sneak back to the private little world I had created for myself. My running away and escaping from home didn't become an everyday occurrence or a serious habit, but I did become emboldened by my success and increased the number of my absences. That confidence was shaken a bit on that fateful day I was summoned to the principal's office.

The principal asked me to sit down and then looked down upon me. "You know it's very important for you to be in school. And it's very important that you go to class. I understand that you've been having some issues with making it all the way from your house to the classroom."

Apathetically, I shrugged.

The school administrator handed me a piece of paper and pencil. "I want you to write one hundred times on this paper, 'I will not skip school' and then hand it back to me."

"I'll give it back right now." I flung the pencil and paper at the surprised principal and then took off out the door. I didn't stop running until I exited the building, navigated the park, and skidded to a stop at my front door, where I used the key to let myself in to enjoy the state of solitude I loved. I felt very proud of myself for controlling the situation. When my mom got home from her teaching job, she let the air out of my balloon very quickly.

"Anything special happen at school today Andy?"

"No." As I shook my head.

"That's not what I heard. I received a very frustrating phone call today at work. Your principal interrupted my job to tell me you've been skipping school and then you followed that up by throwing things at him."

Her voice was much louder at the end than when she began. She also was speaking through clenched teeth. I felt the pride ooze out and the fear ooze in.

"You know what this means, young man?"

"You're gonna whip me?"

"You bet! I want you to know that this is going to hurt me more than it hurts you."

"I don't think so."

At that point in my life, I could have figured out that doing wrong things usually ended up in unpleasant punishment. However, I simply decided that doing wrong things was OK. It was the getting caught part that was the problem and needed to change. From then on I knew they'd be watching me closely, and I'd have to be even sneakier than before. In the end, I never did find a foolproof means to escape detection, but grew stronger in body so that the spankings became almost a laughing matter to me.

After the first round of corporal punishment, my mother tried to find out what motivated her boy to avoid school. I refused to tell her about my inner turmoil. My teacher tried to probe into the matter at school the next day, and I held my tongue again. I figured that if I revealed my pain regarding family matters and my life, I would be acting like a baby and as a first grader I was not a baby anymore and was not going to act like one.

Chapter 5

The Babysitter from Hell

Since my mother was now single, she was forced to work full time. Her job sometimes required her to work overtime as well. That meant that she often had to herd us kids off to a babysitter. Both sets of grandparents lived in the same town, and they both took us kids from time to time, but they weren't up to the challenge of taking care of us all the time. That situation led to an encounter with the babysitter of whom every kid has nightmares.

I got a really bad impression of my new caretaker early on. She made us lie down and take a nap every afternoon. I didn't have a problem with that. The other kids and I weren't extremely delighted with the rules concerning that nap. We had gone down for our usual nap when I decided I needed to use the bathroom. I got up to empty my bladder and a torrent of angry words washed over me.

"But I have to go to the bathroom," I pleaded.

"I don't care. The rule is that you wait until after nap time. Now get back over there and lie down! Now!"

I considered disobeying for a second, but the mean look on the lady's heavy face convinced me that she was not somebody I wanted to mess with. I lay back down and spent the nap time alternating between thinking how badly I needed to use the bathroom and how horrible the babysitter was.

In talking with the other kids afterward, I discovered that some of them had wet their pants during their nap time rather than bring the yells of the babysitter down upon their head by requesting permission to go. These little accidents only brought on more anger from the babysitter as the children were stuck in a no-win situation.

I was used to getting my favorite gourmet spaghetti and meatball meal at my grandmother's house. The cuisine the new babysitter whipped up fell a long distance short of the standard grandma had set.

Between the yelling and the bad food, I was ready to escape again. I discovered a surefire way to make sure I didn't have to put up with the babysitter from hell. If I conveniently missed the bus after school, I wouldn't be able to go to the babysitter's house. In that event, my grandmother would pick me up and keep me at her house. I became very creative in ways to miss the bus.

My frequent failures to board the bus before it departed finally instigated an inquiry from my mother.

"Andy, why do you miss the bus so much? It's not that hard to walk from your class to the bus, is it?"

"No, not really? But, I..."

"Then why can't you get it done?"

I shrugged without thought.

"Now come on Andy. Give me an answer."

"OK, because I want to miss the bus."

"What? Why would you want to miss your bus on purpose?"

"Because I don't want to go over to her house anymore."

"Her? Who's her?"

"The babysitter."

"What are you talking about? What's the matter with the babysitter?"

"Mom, I don't know what's the matter with her, but she seems to take it out on us kids all the time. I hate it over there. She screams all the time, the place is a mess, she doesn't let any of us kids go to the bathroom, and the food stinks."

"She doesn't let you go to the bathroom? The food stinks?"

"How would you like to eat cold hot dogs? Or be forced to eat cold and gritty macaroni and cheese? Most people treat their dogs better than she treats us. And yes, she won't ever let anyone go to the bathroom during nap time."

"Why didn't you tell me Andy?"

"I tried a couple of times, but you didn't listen or believe me. Why can't I just go to grandma's house every day?"

"Andy, I do listen and we have talked about this. It's just too much for your grandma. So, if I find you a different baby sitter, you'll quit missing the bus?"

"Yeah."

"Promise?"

"I promise."

My mother nodded. "OK. I'll start looking tomorrow. I love you Andy. I'm sorry as I didn't realize it was that bad over there. I'll be sure to have a little talk with the babysitter."

"Can I go to grandma's house until you find someone?"

" You really like it at your grandma's house, don't you?"

I nodded. "Yep."

"I can't make you a promise Andy, but I'll talk to grandma tomorrow."

In the end, instead of finding a new babysitter, my mother allowed me to permanently go to my grandma's house after school. As an adult, I came to understand the internal struggle that my mother must have gone through to arrive at that decision. As she wrestled with single parenthood, job pressures, and financial difficulties, she must have wanted to control her own life as much as possible. Of course I didn't understand it completely at the time, but I was very happy to escape from an abusive babysitting environment.

Chapter 6

The Brady Bunch Double Portion

Second grade passed and third grade came, bringing with it some milestone moments. My life was still a teeter-totter ride of up and down cycles with problems at school and the family situation leading the way in causing the downward spirals.

One day I swiped a cigarette and a bottle of cheap liquor from the liquor cabinet at the house and shoved it all into my backpack. I then took off towards the park near our house to meet a friend, carrying the grandiose idea in my head that I'd be considered the coolest kid in school for my actions. I ran to the big picnic shelter with a rock fireplace on the south side of the park. There was a flat landing spot on the top of the fireplace up in the rafters of the roof, which served perfectly as a hiding place for many kids in the neighborhood who needed a private place to smoke or drink. I sat staring at the stolen liquor bottle and cigarette in the backpack waiting to impress my friend once he arrived. I was pumped with excitement and paranoia as my friend arrived and climbed up to see what the grand surprise was. As he looked at the things I had brought, my friend got worried and wasn't quite yet ready to take that path.

"No way!" The other boy called out as he climbed down the fireplace headed back towards his house a few blocks away.

"You're a druggie." I heard my friend yell back at me as he walked away. I sat in silence thinking of everything that just took place.

"Please don't tell anyone!" I yelled back at him.

I had been so excited to impress my friend, but that feeling was crushed as loneliness and rejection quickly swooped in and took hold.

Anger, confusion, and the feeling of defeat burned within me as I climbed down and slowly completed the walk of shame back to my house to return the bottle of liquor. Along the way I hurled the unlit cigarette on the ground and angrily smashed it with my foot.

My friend and the other kids at school weren't quite ready for that much excitement. Just as I feared, my friend told a good number of classmates, and my image was tarnished a bit that next school day. Not really wanting to be called a "druggie" by my fellow classmates, I cooled it with the thievery of those forbidden substances - until fifth grade.

Other things brought turmoil to me that school year. I struggled mightily in art class that year and the fault was not totally my own. Whenever the students were required to create a project to be taken home to their parents, I felt I had to do two, one for each of my parents, since they no longer shared a home. In my hurry to get them done on time, I had to cut corners, preventing my work from being the best it could have been with the amount of time given. It didn't seem fair to me that the art teacher didn't take into consideration my circumstances and cut me some slack. I was convinced an art teacher should grade on effort.

I was mad and told my mother.

"She doesn't get it!"

Knowing my mom taught a little art herself I knew she would support me. To my satisfaction, my mother completely agreed and talked with the teacher about the struggles children of divorce sometimes go through to please both parents.

A failing grade in English killed whatever desire and motivation I had to succeed in the scholastic setting. I discovered that apathy was an effective way to ward off pain.

One day I decided that since it seemed more fun living with my dad than my mom, I was going to change my custodial arrangement myself without help from a judge. I packed my belongings that would fit into a big duffel bag and started peddling my bicycle toward my father's house as fast as I could go with the burden of the large bag.

One block from my destination, my mother drove past me and slammed on the brakes. I remember that she pulled the duffel bag out of my grasp with one hand while she was shifting the car into park with the other. Faster than I had ever seen her move, she bolted out of the car, popped the trunk open and threw the bag inside. I could tell from the look on her face that it was not the time to be rebellious and utter any type of protest. She grabbed the bicycle and threw it into the trunk as well.

"Get in the car. We're going home."

Once again my plan for my life was foiled. I even felt guilty at my attempt because I knew my mother's life as a single parent was tough and I was part of the problem and not the solution.

Fourth grade brought an even bigger event. My mother decided to tie the knot with her boyfriend, the father of three boys. Fortune again was on my side when my new stepfather turned out to be a very kind loving man. I respected my new parent as someone who helped my mother out and took care of her, my sister, and myself. In a way, I felt rich because I had two homes, two sets of parents, four sets of grandparents, which translated into a whole lot of people to give me Christmas presents.

Despite those advantages, I had mixed emotions about my mother's marriage. I even had some difficulty at school trying to explain why my mother never took my stepdad's last name. It made a complex family situation even more so. I realized there was no way my initial family was ever going to get back together. My long held dream of reunion died within me.

The chemistry with the new stepbrothers wasn't as good as the relationships I had with my adopted brothers at my dad's house. Many times fights would break out between us. We didn't punch each other, but sometimes a wall received the brunt of someone's angry fist. Yelling at each other was quite common. The three new brothers were going to take some getting used to.

It's not easy for five kids, born of two different sets of parents, to live in harmony. It's even more difficult when those kids are brought together as part of a merger of two broken homes and each is walking down their own path devoid of Biblical ethics and moral guidance.

This new family situation was the start of both a blissful and a stressful road. Unfortunately, the new dynamics added to the teeter-totter effect that plagued me. One day it was good, but the next day, someone (sometimes myself) would get out of control and disturb the peace. My mom and step-dad tried desperately to get all of us kids to get along, but it was like herding cats.

Whenever one of the kids received a present or something new, usually one of the other kids would consider that they weren't getting treated fairly and would protest angrily. After the parents grew weary of the sibling civil war, they enrolled the group in family counseling.

Despite all of that, some days I found my new family situation awesome as all of us boys played hockey or basketball together. Once again, sports seemed to be the glue that held my world together.

Despite having a total of five stepbrothers, my sister Sonja and I, remained close throughout the divorce and both remarriages. She helped me get through a lot of tough days. The two of us played board games as kids and later in high school went to a lot of the same parties together.

I considered that my life was like the kids on the 1970s Brady Bunch show. The trouble was I had two separate merged families to adjust to. Sometimes I found it to be exhausting and confusing to live one week with a certain set of rules and then return to the other parents' house where suddenly a whole new set of people and rules controlled me. I came to the conclusion over the years that it was easier to go off on my own. I was independent, so I had no qualms or fears about heading out into the town to meet friends, or simply walk, bike, or roller skate around the town.

Sometimes I'd hide out at my maternal grandparents' house. They owned a cement block company which provided really cool places to play inside and out. The terrain around the business included huge sand and rock piles, the perfect hangout for an adventuresome boy who climbed, jumped, dug and biked all over the piles.

I loved to construct forts out of the heavy cement blocks lying around. That secluded environment and play material provided my troubled self an escape from all the chaos that seemed to surround me everywhere else. On days when my cousins were around, we would all pretend to run the family business between the house and office phones. The big black drainage tubes coiled together provided a perfect hide-and-seek course. My favorite activity was walking up the huge conveyor belt that stretched high above the silo near the cement truck loading side of the plant. Here I would be able to see the entire town. The fun part about this area was no one was ever up here except for pigeons. Instead of walking back down the conveyor belt, I had a very genius way of maneuvering through the stairways, iron support beams, grated walkways, cinder block piles and machinery to make it to the bottom and out the opposite side of the massive plant. The trek was surely a boy's ultimate obstacle course dream.

Chapter 7

Speaking of Sports

One reason that I was angry much of the time involved my frustration with loving sports, but not having a full time dad to play with me and coach me consistently in the basics. My father was a good athlete who had played basketball in college. It seemed to me that he was proficient in whatever sport he dabbled with. Whenever I was with dad, he and I always seemed to be involved in a competitive contest of some type. However, the daily presence of a father-like-coach was obviously frustrating by his absence.

Sports had been fun in the past, but became even more important to me as I grew older. The father-son duo of my dad and I began to grow apart, and less and less time was spent together playing sports. It became so serious when we were together, as the simple fun was replaced with a boot camp like atmosphere. The thrill of competition and the physical activity provided the adrenaline rush I craved and an outlet for my boundless energy. I was short, quick and strong for my size. The structure of sporting programs brought some needed stability to my life as well.

One of the perks of participation in sports was that it gave me a chance to earn my dad's approval. That drove me in my efforts to compete because I wanted my dad to be proud of me. My dad gave me the choice of wrestling or basketball, but he required that I get involved in one of them. No child was to sit around our house and dare mention that they were bored. My "new" brothers in my dad's mixed family were both freestyle wrestlers, so to be with my brothers, I chose wrestling.

I wasn't exactly enamored with wrestling when I began, but I did want to win favor from my dad. After being involved in the sport for a short time, I came to the conclusion that wrestling gave me a chance to get into fights and release some of my hostility without getting into trouble. I referred to it as organized fighting.

Alas, my wrestling career was short lived. To this day I remember vividly the day the wrestling relationship died. It happened one weekend when I was staying at my dad's place. My stepbrothers were going to wrestle in a freestyle tournament in a neighboring town, so my dad entered me into the tournament as well.

He woke us boys up early the morning of the tournament, telling us that they were leaving in thirty minutes. He had already packed the food and drinks for the day, so all I had to do was get dressed and pack something to keep me busy when I wasn't wrestling. Us four "guys" headed to the tournament at 7:30 a.m. After an hour of driving, we arrived and found the place to weigh in. A big crowd of kids gathered to scan the pairings to see who they'd be wrestling against.

My younger brother and I, who happened to be in the same weight class, finally got up to the big white board that held our bracket. I found my name and then did a double take. If both my brother and I won our first round, we would wrestle each other in the next round. One of us could be out of the tournament in the second round. We went back to where our dad waited.

"I'm wrestling against my brother!" I explained to my dad.

My dad's face showed his dismay. "What? No way. I'm going to see someone and get this changed immediately."

He left us sitting in the bleachers to find tournament officials to whom he could lodge a complaint. A little while later, he returned, wearing an unhappy look that conveyed the obvious. We were going to wrestle each other. It became a very awkward moment between us brothers as neither wanted to wrestle the other. At home was fine as most brothers wrestle and play together, but this was serious as one of us would be the loser that day. That was a thought neither of us wanted to entertain.

I figured this was going to be a fight of the century. I wasn't about to lose to my brother. My opponent had the same look of determination as I did. We didn't even talk to each other for the next hour as we both waited for the match to begin.

When the time came to wrestle, our dad was not in either corner. He had found other dads to handle the coaching duties because he couldn't coach both of us at the same time, and he didn't want either of us to be favored by having dad in their corner.

To thicken the plot, I saw my mother in the stands. I could hear her yelling at me to get fired up. I saw trouble brewing because having my dad and my mother both at one of my matches was not a good thing, especially when my opponent was my dad's adopted son, my own stepbrother. I hoped that my mom and dad didn't get into their own wrestling match in front of all of those people.

When the ref blew his whistle, the two of us brothers met in the center of the mat and shook hands. I was ready. I was not going to lose in front of both my parents. If I won, maybe they would talk to each other without arguing.

The whistle blew, and the match began. I got the initial takedown plus two more points for a near fall. I was ahead 4 – 0 right out of the gate, and the score stayed that way until halfway through the second period. Then I got put on my back for a near fall giving my brother two points, making the score 4 – 2. The last period started, and again I got taken down to the mat, yielding another four points and losing my lead. With just a few seconds left in the match, I broke away from my brother and earned one point for an escape. I took my brother down for two more points placing me back in front with a score of 7 – 6. The final seconds were ticking away with me in control. I simply had to maintain that control to win. Then the unforgettable happened, I heard my mother yell something at me. For some careless reason I looked up into the stands to try to find her.

While my concentration was diverted, my brother took advantage. Just before time expired, he slipped out of my grasp and managed to reverse our positions, earning him two points for a takedown and the victory.

I had lost. I couldn't believe it. The way it had happened in such an embarrassing turn of events was one I would never forget. I felt as though the world was over. I made up my mind, there on the spot, that I would never be humiliated like that again. I was done with wrestling. I was mad at my mother. I was mad at my dad. I was even mad at my brother. I wanted no part of something that I couldn't control, and I obviously couldn't control wrestling.

A year later, I did come out of retirement to wrestle (without preparation) in a tournament. My brother and I left to visit his family up in northern Minnesota for a vacation. We loved visiting them as they had access to some of the best fishing lakes in Minnesota. One of my more amusing memories up north was when my brother and I threw frogs into a culvert connecting two lakes in an attempt to net bass fish as they jumped out of the water towards the frogs for an easy meal.

We soon discovered a wrestling tournament scheduled to take place in the town we were staying. I entered despite not training for it. In my first match I led 3-2 after the first period. Unfortunately, during the second period, I dislocated my elbow breaking a fall. After visiting the hospital, where the doctor put on my cast, I discovered how hard it was to fish with one arm the rest of the vacation. I never wrestled an official match again.

After dropping wrestling, I took up basketball. Not only did I find I really liked it, but I was pretty good at it as well. I was not very tall, but I was extremely quick.

Many young boys get a chance to get away to summer camp where they fellowship and play with other kids from many different places. I'd never had the opportunity to do the "canoeing, swimming, and poison ivy" camp thing.

I did, however, get to participate in something that many kids who live in agricultural areas get to experience: working on a farm. I loved the outside work. I loved lugging bales of hay and straw to a flatbed and watching the bales pile up toward the sky like giant Lego building blocks. Picking up rocks was a pretty cool pastime as well, as I helped clean the fields from the pesky stones that could damage farm equipment. I even had the experience of helping milk cows on a dairy farm. Pulling weeds in between the soybean plants was not as pleasant a chore, but I even enjoyed that menial task also. I thrived on being active. I always felt a sense of accomplishment at the end of a hard day's work. And the outdoors always made me feel alive.

So while some of my friends were off singing around a campfire in the summer at camp, I spent the time, between my fourth and fifth grade year, busy being a farmer's assistant.

When I reached the fifth grade, I finally got to go to my first camp, the opportunity of a lifetime. My dad signed me up to attend a basketball camp. Although the majority of the athletes were from Minnesota, the camp hosted over 500 kids from all around the country.

I was pumped to attend my first camp, but after arriving and finding myself in such a crowd of unfamiliar boys, I started having second thoughts. I was alone in the midst of an ocean of strangers for the first time in my life, and I immediately felt out of place.

The only time I felt comfortable was when the coaches had me playing or scrimmaging on the basketball court. It was there that I felt I shined. I was a defensive whirlwind. As fast as greased lightning, I could steal the ball from even the best offensive players. I loved that part of camp, but when I walked off the court, the insecurities kicked in again and made me homesick for a familiar environment.

I absolutely hated the camp experience when I wasn't playing hoops. The hours of the weeklong camp seemed to tick by so slowly in the evening hours. I often cried at night, wanting so badly to have my father come back and take me home. I phoned home the first night.

"Dad, I wanna go home." I fought away the tears.

"You just got there!" My dad replied, surprised by the phone call.

"I know, but I wanna go home."

"Why?"

"I hate it here."

"Andy, you love basketball. How could you hate basketball camp? You're getting great coaching and having great competition too, I'm sure. This doesn't make any sense. Just stick it out Andy. Give it a chance. I'm not coming to get you."

Every night for the first three days, I spent time on the phone pleading with my father to come get me. On the third night, my dad informed me that he had spoken to the camp director, and set up a meeting between us both.

"I want you to sit down and simply talk to him like you're talking to me. If you're still not happy, I'll come get you."

"OK." I cautiously replied.

My father's last words were, "listen to him."

With a bit of trepidation, I walked toward the office. It didn't help that the director's office was down a long dimly lit hallway. I hesitated to enter but finally worked up enough courage to walk inside. To my surprise, the man was very friendly and upbeat.

"I know what you're going through, Andy. I had a similar experience with home sickness when I was a kid."

"Really?"

"Yep. When I pulled out of my shell and just let myself enjoy those other kids instead of being intimidated by them, my problem went away. I promise that if you give a little effort to be fully involved on and off the court, you won't want to go home."

Reluctantly, knowing my dad was strongly urging me to stay the full week, I agreed. As I trudged back to my bunk, I decided to just quit whining and do as much as I could, both on and off the court. I'd play with the other boys. I'd hang out by the television and the snack area and make jokes. Most of all, I'd play basketball as hard as I could.

I put his plan into implementation. The next day, I found myself laughing so hard that it hurt. I realized that the director was right on. I had forgotten about home and had the time of my life.

The coaches expressed that they were amazed at my hustle and prowess on defense. In every game the coaches assigned me to guard the other team's best ball-handler, knowing I would disrupt that boy's game and thus the other team's offense.

The remaining days of the camp flew by, and the last day arrived, as did my dad and stepmom to take me home. All of the campers gathered on the floor of the big gym for the presentation of awards and certificates. The wrap-around balcony above the gym was full of proud parents waving and flashing cameras, sharing the special experience with their children.

I looked all around and finally found my dad, standing there with a prideful smile. It felt wonderful. I turned back to my new friends who sat and laughed with me on the gym floor as the director announced the winners of the awards.

When the director's voice on the loudspeaker echoed, "Andy Peterson", I thought I heard wrong. My new friends all cheered and pushed me toward the director and the awards table. On my way up, I realized that I had won one of only three highly coveted hustle awards. This award meant everything to me.

As the boys began to disperse after the ceremony, bound for their homes and regular lives again, I revisited the last seven days of memories in my head. From begging to go home at the beginning, I'd arrived at a point where I was sad to be leaving. I was hooked and wanted to do camp all over again. I started making plans to go back the next year, and counting the days until that camp started.

Unfortunately, the lesson I learned of how adjusting my attitude made situations in my life better, didn't carry over to my life back home. My established bad attitudes continued to get me into trouble.

My elementary school.

The park where I hid before sneaking back home to skip school.

My stepbrothers and I showing off our wrestling tournament trophies and brackets.

My mother and I.

Wearing my hustle award at basketball camp.

Me running the high hurdles during a track and field meet in high school.

Me in my varsity football uniform with my dad.

My dad, stepmom, sister, stepbrothers and I.

My mom, stepdad, sister, stepbrothers and I.

Our cabin near the lake where all my high school parties were held.

Edge of the Grand Canyon during my solo trip out west where I slept in my car.

Winter camping in Rocky Mountain National Park during my solo trip out west.

Entrance road to Roxborough State Park, location of Carpenter's Peak Trail.

Carpenter's Peak trailhead near the visitors' center of Roxborough State Park.

Flight for Lift helicopter rescue team in action.

My bloodied hiking shorts.

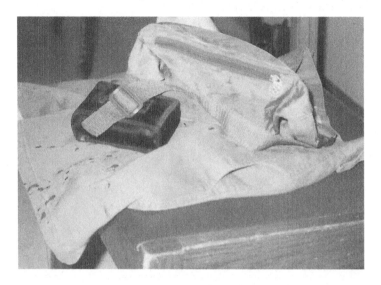

Me in the hospital on the first day of recovery.

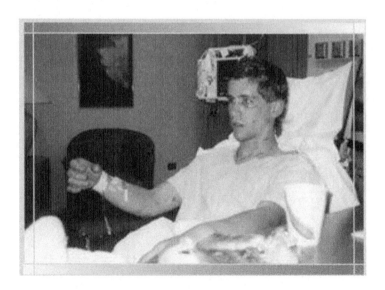

Me recovering from rabies vaccination.

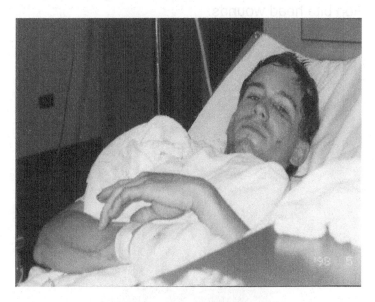

Me recovering from plastic surgery.

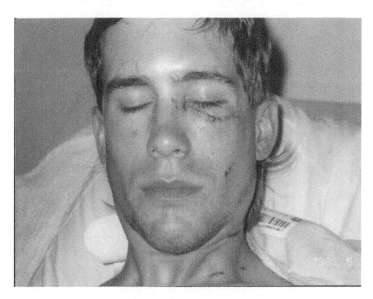

Me showing the record number of staples to close lion bite head wounds.

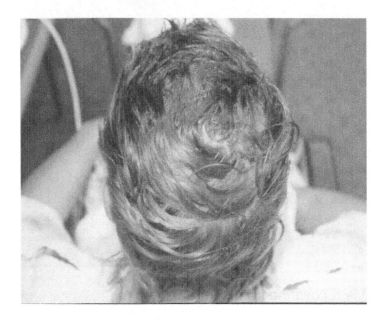

Me showing the claw marks and puncture wounds from the mountain lion.

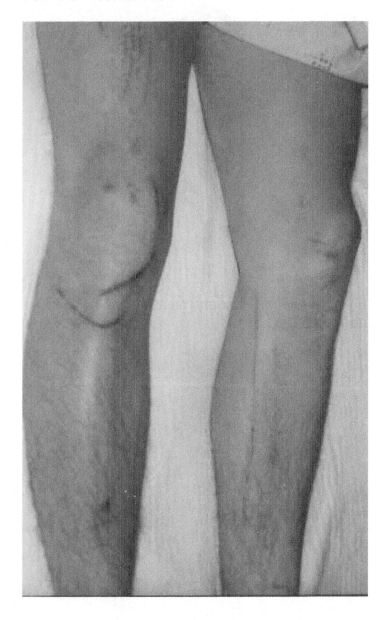

The day I was being released from the hospital.

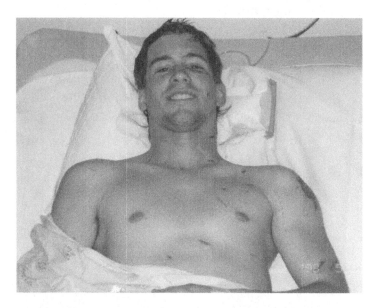

My mother and I after my release from the hospital.

Lion located on the Colorado mountain ridge (look near bottom of large middle tree).

Lion jumping away from us on the mountain ridge.

My father, stepmother and I before my wedding.

My mother, stepfather and I before my wedding.

Me marrying my best friend Cortney Aug. 11, 2001.

Holding my two precious children on Father's Day 2009.

My children and I during a T.V. interview in 2011.

Fall 2011 family picture.

Fall 2012 goofy family picture.

Speaking at a Wild Game Dinner.

Speaking at an outreach event.

Speaking at a Sunday church service.

Chapter 8

Stuck in the Middle

I returned to experimenting with alcohol and tobacco. I was now buying cigarettes from my stepdad's oldest son for ten cents apiece. Both of us were happy with that arrangement, since I really didn't have another good way to obtain them. The only other place I knew where to obtain cigarettes was an old cigarette vending machine in a hotel doorway at the edge of town. About once a week, I would reach my hand way up into the front of the machine and grab a pack or two. With a stolen bottle here and there from the family liquor cabinet, cigarettes, and staying out late, I thought I had it made.

Fifth grade brought a momentous event to my life. I finally got the desire of my heart, the opportunity to live with my father. I didn't have to run away this time, but was given permission by my mother to move. My reason in making the change in residence was to get more freedom. Another reason was to get away from some of the conflict and fighting with my stepbrothers at my mom's house. I'm sure my mother was a bit weary of that conflict as well, in addition to the fatigue caused by trying to keep me and my stepbrothers in line.

In sixth grade, I began the practice of putting a mark on my bedroom door frame every time I got in a fight or found a new girlfriend. It seemed as though I was having a hard time choosing between love and war. Like many boys, I took great pride in my success with girls. I considered them trophies, and the more trophies in my case the better. I also prided myself on my hands and the quick punches they could throw. As a result, I ended up with thirteen marks on my wall in each category before the school year ended.

I squandered another learning opportunity during this time frame. One of the girlfriend marks on the wall belonged to someone who was special to me, but not special enough to stay true to. When I cheated on her by kissing one of her friends, I basically signed the death warrant on that relationship. She let me have it verbally and then with a quick angry slap, she stormed out of my house. I stood in my room alone, listening to the slamming door and feeling the sting on my cheek, I felt very little regret or remorse. Over the years and all the family and life changes, I simply hardened my heart and vowed to do unto others before they did unto me.

Chapter 9

New Meaning to term High School

The summer after sixth grade wound to a close, and seventh grade was on the horizon. I was fired up for this new, advanced grade because I would now go to the big high school where my sister and stepbrothers attended. I'd be going from the elementary school where my sixth grade class was king of the hill to a building where we'd be the runts of the litter. That could have been very intimidating, but I had lots of friends in upper grades because of my brothers and sister, so I totally looked forward to the new experience.

Me and my stepbrother who was in the same grade, spent hours cutting pictures of trucks, liquor bottles, cool camping scenes, sports items, popular music bands and pretty girls out of magazines to decorate the inside of our lockers. Such a practice was a school tradition especially in the younger grades.

One of the milestone events in my life in the seventh grade actually happened to my father, although at the time I was unaware of what impact it would have in my life in the future. My dad became a born-again Christian, resulting in his becoming stricter in his parenting approach, causing my strategy of moving in with dad for more freedom to backfire. Dad began to attend church regularly, and he expected his sons to join the family at the services.

I was almost bored to death by church. A testosterone laden youngster with energy to burn suffers when being put into a situation where he has to sit and listen to someone drone on about a topic that is not particularly interesting to him. My dad's devotion to Jesus Christ did not seem like a good thing at the time, but in retrospect was an event of paramount importance.

Seventh grade was going well for me. I was doing okay in my classes and loved all the football and basketball games with the older high school kids. One daring adventure I enjoyed with friends was sneaking through the custodian's offices down into the tunnels below the high school and running through them. The riskiest times of sneaking into the tunnels were during the basketball or swimming competitions when hundreds of people were attending. There, the tunnels led to a window below the diving board of the indoor school pool.

In addition to cruising Main Street where kids drove their cars back and forth, the big hangout in town for the kids was the arcade at the local shopping mall. I loved the arcade and hung out there as often as I could. One night towards the end of seventh grade, I was at the arcade with a couple of friends.

"I got some marijuana," one of my friends said.

"Yeah, right," the other friend replied.

The first friend pulled a clear plastic bag out of his pocket and showed us, causing my other friends' eyebrows to rise to the occasion.

"Wow! Where did you get that?" I asked.

"My big brother. Wanna try some?"

"Where?" I asked.

The boy pointed to some open fields a short distance from the arcade.

The three of us boys walked until we came upon a small section of brush and trees that would hide our activities. My heart beat rapidly as I sat on the ground, feeling both paranoid and excited at the same time at my pending initiation into the world of drugs.

My skeptical friend and I watched in anticipation and awe as our adventurous friend showed us how to roll a joint. Soon we were all puffing and inhaling the euphoria causing cannabis. We spent the next several minutes tucked in the trees in the field, sharing that one large joint until every last bit of it was burned. We then sat staring at each other waiting for some marvelous feeling to overcome us.

After nothing seemed to happen, we got up and walked back to the mall with disappointment, not realizing the hallucinatory effects were creeping up on us. When we arrived back at the arcade, all the flashing lights and noises soon made it clear that a high from the marijuana was indeed real. The thought that no one, other than my friends and myself, knew why we were laughing at everyone and everything, was thrilling.

What I didn't know was that my brief introduction to pot would lead to a habitual routine that would become a proverbial monkey on my back daily for twelve years. After alternating through paranoia, and laughter, we all developed a case of the munchies!

I walked across the mall's parking lot over to the nearby McDonald's restaurant, digging deep into my pockets with hopes that I had enough for the fifty-nine cent burger. I found a single dollar bill, so I walked into the restaurant and up to the counter. When the clerk set my bag of food on the counter, I laid my bill with George Washington's picture on it onto the counter to pay. The clerk immediately walked away to the drive-up window to help another customer, leaving the dollar bill near the food bag on the shiny counter in front of me, a now confused and tempted customer.

I wondered why the clerk didn't take the money as I stared at the greenback that I had desperately dug for earlier. I glanced once more at the busy cashier, and then swooped up money and bag of food and darted for the door. Laughing as though I had pulled off an ingenious heist, I walked back to the Arcade, eating my delicious hamburger with one hand and gripping my dollar bill with the other.

My conscience wrestled with me a little. *That was wrong!* I fought back. *Why? No one saw it! Plus, I have a dollar more to spend on a game.*

The next morning, I got a lesson in the difference between living in a big city where hardly anyone knows their next door neighbor and a smaller town where people know just about everyone. When I came out to the kitchen to grab some breakfast, my dad confronted me. In a quiet, yet firm tone, he said, "Hey son, go get into the car and come to town with me."

My dad didn't say anything further as the car coasted through the streets of Hutchinson, but I knew something was up, especially when the car pulled into the McDonald's parking lot. My heart raced and practically beat out of my chest when my dad turned to me with a look of disappointment written all over his face.

"The manager at this McDonald's is a friend of mine. I got a call late last night from him about you ordering food and walking out without paying. That's stealing son. You can find yourself in jail for a stunt like that. I'll tell you this once, go in there, apologize face-to-face like a man, and make it right."

I was busted. With bowed head, I shamefully walked into the restaurant to personally apologize to the manager for my theft and to pay for the burger. I then had to face my dad once more for the return trip.

"Trust is something you have to earn, son. Once you break that trust, it takes time to gain it back - if it's even possible to get it back. Think about that."

"Yes, sir." I replied quietly as I kept my head bowed and fidgeted with my hands the whole trip home.

In the summer between my seventh and eighth grade year, I have a distinct memory involving all of my stepbrothers. My mother and stepfather announced that they were taking a lengthy vacation without us kids. To enhance the good news was the fact that the oldest boy would be in charge of us younger ones.

Since my mother was out of town, I wouldn't be leaving my dad's to make my normal parental weekend visit to my mom's house, but I was not going to miss out on the fun my siblings there had planned. My adopted brothers who lived with my dad also got in on the fun. We all managed to concoct a story about doing something else for the evening, so we could host our own parties.

My mother lived in a four story home (including the basement and attic), which allowed all six of us boys to plan smaller parties within one huge party, which would be worthy of a movie scene. With all of us boys spread out over seven grades, we decided to have each grade party on its own level of the house with the older kids getting the best floors.

The party started out wonderfully, in my mind. I exulted in helping to bring together one of the biggest parties my town had seen in years. But just like in the movies, things started going sour after the celebrating got a bit out of hand. Huge messes appeared as items in the house started breaking and drinks and food spilled from their containers. And some items such as VHS movies and music cassettes tapes disappeared.

For a minute, my mind started processing what was going on and questioning our wisdom in launching this massive party. The people I'd considered my friends and whom I trusted, were trashing my mother's house and belongings. My guilt rose as I realized my parents had worked hard to get what they had and these party goers seemed to have no regard or respect. The fact that punishment would probably follow my mother's return also rained on my parade as I considered the consequences.

However, the worries about the house and having to pay the price were not nearly enough to cause me to call a halt to the good times being had by all. Besides, my other brothers were doing it as well, so my parents couldn't single me out. Since I wasn't in charge, I couldn't stop things even if I was so inclined, which I wasn't.

The mega party opened a far more dangerous door than I ever realized. I had gotten a taste of popularity, and I liked it - a lot. I saw the opportunity to make more friends, throw more parties, and take advantage of more opportunities to get high. The mega party had set off an explosion of ideas in my head and from those ideas, eventually came a regular party at my parents' cabin on the lake on the weekends. I had thought the gathering in the house was huge at the time. The crowd that arrived to party at the lake and bonfire was even bigger.

As the party became more infamous, so did the crowd and the resulting behavior. Kids from other towns were now talking about the regular weekend cabin parties as more and more showed up with each passing party. Sound carries very well across water. When a group of teenagers gather with alcohol and music, the sound level goes up exponentially. Soon the neighbors on the lake began complaining of the noise and of the road being overrun by lines of cars, kids out of control, and huge fires.

I began to feel the strain of all this. In spite of all my selfishness, there was still a sense of right and wrong in myself, and I knew that this would eventually lead to trouble. My worries were proven right when I saw racist signs burned on the ground, fences being destroyed, dog houses burned, and a travel trailer destroyed so completely that it looked as if a bomb had been detonated inside.

It came to a point that the cops were being called every weekend. As soon as I heard the sirens and cars roaring down the street, I knew it was time to make a hasty exit. I had been to the lake enough times to know my way around and always managed to get away by sprinting down the beach through the trees along the shoreline. Although I still had a sense of right and wrong, I was certainly not brave enough to speak out against the wrong and jeopardize my new found popularity. I was now completely out of control and running down a very dangerous unstable "fast-lane" in life.

I knew the dangers of seeking the approval of my peers, but I wasn't overly concerned with them because I found the feeling of being popular a marvelous upgrade of my social status. Sliding back down the ladder was simply not acceptable.

Scores of cool kids were coming from not only my school, but from other towns. I knew only a few of them, but they all knew me. My reputation preceded me. I, Andy Peterson, was being treated as a big man on campus, and I was soaking it all in. I had what I thought every boy in high school wanted, based on what I saw in the movies from Hollywood. But, like so many of those people in the movies, I was not a hero. I thought I was nice and kind and didn't see myself as a bully, but my actions were entirely self-serving.

The day came when my illegal activity caught up with me. I found myself standing in front of a judge facing an underage drinking charge, which was a misdemeanor. None of my friends I made partying, or who patted my back to tell me how cool I was, were anywhere to be seen.

Standing in front of a judge marked a turning point in my life. It yielded to a dangerous road ahead. I could have made the choice to turn around and to straighten my life up. Or I could have chosen to keep going toward the same out-of-control destination. This misdemeanor was a minor speed bump in the road. I dug in deep and kept forging ahead.

My life proceeded in a fairly predictable manner through the next few years. Partying, getting high, sports, and girls dominated my life and my viewpoint of the world.

My junior year of high school gave another opportunity of mischief presented itself. I had discovered I could successfully sneak in and out my bedroom window to freedom at night, even though my father's bedroom was directly above me. In order to keep the window from closing completely shut, I stuck a pillow between the window and the sill. Not only did that keep the window open so I could get back in, but it helped keep the cold air out and muffled the sound of the window being opened and closed.

When I snuck out, I usually headed toward the park near the cemetery and met up with a couple friends to drink and smoke dope. Sometimes, when they couldn't get out, I would sit in the park alone.

One morning I discovered I wasn't as clever as I thought. My dad pulled me aside.

"Where did you go last night when you snuck out?"

"What are you talking about?"

"Andy, don't play dumb with me. You went out last night. What were you doing?"

"What makes you think I went out?"

"I watched you leave."

"Oh." I hesitated.

"I just went out to get some food."

"What's the matter with the food in the fridge?"

"And I forgot something at..."

My dad interrupted. "Andy. You lied to me about sneaking out. Why should I believe anything you say? Things are going to have to change around here, because I just can't trust you anymore."

My dad's words were no idle threat. Homework was now supervised at the dining room table. Phone time with friends was limited to ten minutes per day. No going out and staying out late privileges. Everything was now micro-managed. I was now on a chain and didn't like the way things had changed. I didn't pause to realize my dad was setting ground rules to protect me from hurting others and myself. That he was trying to protect my future. What I did know was that I had an escape, my mother's house. I decided to change primary residences once again and move back in with my mother. That side of the family had less rules and provided more freedom. I played the game I was dealt. And I played it well. I only had two more years of high school to enjoy, and I knew now that I'd have more freedom to do that if I was living with her.

I also started looking at colleges that I might attend. High on my list of qualifications for a college was the number of party friends I could find there. After all, my adopted older brother walked away from a full scholarship to wrestle at the Naval Academy to go to a school located in Wisconsin known for its great parties. He was doing fine there so what was the problem with a little partying? There was a university about an hour away from my home town where many of my friends had chosen to go to party, and get an education in their spare time. I hastily took advantage of an opportunity to visit the campus and stay with my adopted brother who was visiting friends in their dorm for one night.

Shortly after I arrived, I found out that they were going to party it up that night. I thought it was awesome for an eleventh grader to get to go college parties as if I were one of them. It didn't take long after the partying started that my drinking got out of control. After I was already inebriated, someone informed me that the girl I was dating at the time was staying across town. Drunk from playing a dangerous binge drinking game with my adopted brother and his friends in their dorm room, I stood up, "I'm going to see her."

My adopted brother shook his head firmly. "No way! You're too drunk and aren't going to drive anywhere. Now sit down."

I obeyed, mainly because I knew I could go down the hall to the bathroom and sneak out later in the night. And that's exactly what I did. However, the door I exited was not the front door as I had thought, but was actually the back door of the dorms.

I staggered around, looking for the spot I had parked my mother's car I had driven to the campus. When I figured out that I had come out the wrong door, I became angry and started wandering around the building with my head down, trying to figure out what I was going to do. I was now even more determined to complete my secret mission. My body crashed right into the front of a car. When I glanced up and saw it was very similar to my mother's, I decided to try my key in the door lock. The door unlocked.

The popping noise of the door unlocking let me know that I was in luck. After jumping in, I realized that I possibly could be taking another person's vehicle and I'd be guilty of grand theft auto. I didn't think about it for long, muttering to myself. *"Doesn't matter. I'll bring it right back."*

I drove off, much too inebriated to handle a car proficiently and responsibly. I risked death, my own and that of innocent parties, as I began driving like an Indy 500 racer, speeding around corners towards the other end of town. I slowed as I came to two big orange construction signs blocking the street.

I knew I had to get across a busy highway to get to where my girlfriend was staying. I wasn't going to let a couple of hunks of metal keep us apart, so I maneuvered around the large orange signs clearly labeled, "Do Not Enter! Road Closed!" The road they were blocking turned out to be a downhill one-way street, and I was going the wrong way towards a busy highway. Blue and red lights pierced through the darkness behind me and penetrated inside my car through my rear window. Despite being drunk, I realized I was busted for being drunk and behind the wheel.

If only I listened to my brother. He has to be looking for me by now. How I wish I could take back my stupid, dangerous, selfish, decision to make this trip. Wow, I could have killed someone, even myself.

The only good news was that I was innocent of grand theft auto. The car really was my mom's. However, I was handcuffed, placed in the back of the police car, and hauled unceremoniously to the police station where my blood alcohol measured the legally intoxicated level of 0.21.

The male officer had harsh words for me concerning how dangerous my little joy ride could have been if he hadn't stopped me prior to reaching the highway at the end of the road.

Full of pride, I stood yelling at the officer about having a right to make one phone call. The officer stood firm on not allowing any calls at that time. He placed me on a chair in a room filled with other officer's desks and walked out. I always seemed to use my charm even in the worst conditions. On the other side of the room a female officer sat at her desk and watched the proceedings.

I quickly gained favor with the female officer. She had a phone in hand dialing my adopted brother's dorm room number for me when the male officer returned.

He grabbed the phone, slammed it down and rebuked her sternly. "I said no calls." As he glared back at me.

Later that night sitting in the police station after failing the sobriety test, I had to face my mother and stepfather who had come to get me in the middle of the night. I referred to the trip home as "the ride of shame."

The next day my dad drove over to my mother's house so he and my mother could have a little heart-to-heart talk with me, their out-of-control troublesome son. I had hoped one day to bring my parents back together, but this wasn't the reunion I visualized. I also learned that my mother had called my dad the night before asking if he would go get me, since I was in jail for driving under the influence (DUI). My dad had refused and told my mother that the night spent in jail would be a good lesson for me. In retrospect, my mother should have left me there for the night; I might have learned a lesson or two.

By the end of the conversation, I had played the "victim of divorce" card so skillfully that I avoided major discipline from my parents. I didn't fare so well with the authorities. I lost my license to drive for one year, and received a fine of one thousand dollars and a sentence for community service. I spent ten brutal days cutting brush along a mosquito infested lake shore to fulfill the service part of my punishment. That was not a pastime that I had any desire to return to ever again, to put it mildly. I truly felt punished in this situation. To this day I wonder what would have happened if I'd made it onto that highway.

My "fast-lane" style of living had to slow down. My parents set up some rules and the justice system did as well, but soon enough I was back in the "fast-lane." Even the humility of begging for rides from classmates for a year didn't slow me down. Having no license did however force me to find new ways to smoke pot as my habit and favorite pastime was to drive around the lakes and countryside on the outskirts of town getting high.

Sports continued to play a big role in my life. I played on the varsity football team despite my shorter size. I even won an iron man fitness contest. A couple of my more vivid memories from high school involved football games. In one game, I caught a fifty yard touchdown pass. In another game, I took a kickoff and weaved my way through the wannabe defensive tacklers into the open field. Just when I thought I was going to take it all the way to the end zone, a big linebacker slammed into me from the blind side, and launched me into the air. Gravity pulled me back to the ground where I tumbled into and under the opponents' bench. Dazed, I got up and started running off in the wrong direction as the opponent's teammates yelled and pointed in the opposite direction.

In track, the coach came up with a unique strategy for me to excel in the high hurdles. I was low enough to the ground that I could literally run through the hurdles and not break stride. It wasn't a pretty sight to see me knocking over hurdle after hurdle, but that technique allowed me to be competitive with those tall, long-legged jumpers who typically excelled in the hurdle races. Surprisingly, I even won a good number of those races. I loved the speed of running track. And I loved the adrenaline rush I felt as I ran. Little did I know, one day I'd be running for my life from a powerful mountain lion.

Chapter 10

Go West Young Man

Throughout high school and into college, I talked a lot about going out west to live. I was captivated by the west ever since my mom, stepdad, sister, and stepbrothers went on a weeklong rafting trip down the Colorado River the summer after fifth grade. The mountains fascinated me as did the vastness of the terrain along with the trails, and especially the snow skiing. I bragged to anyone who would listen to my dream about moving to that part of the country. I loved the outdoors, and felt the west would offer me a chance to be myself without the pressure of family and friends to mold me into someone I wasn't.

In the outdoors alone with nature, I felt understood. The trees and bushes were welcome friends. The animals and cool breezes never pressured me. Out in the wide open country I never had to explain myself to anyone.

Minnesota offered its share of outdoor beauty, but my family was part of the equation there. As much as I loved them, I was convinced I couldn't live my entire life under their pressures and rules. I had struggled throughout my youth with the broad spectrum and weight of rules from both sides of my family, school and society. I wanted away from it all.

Trying to conform to others perception of what I should be taxed me both physically and emotionally. For a man of the outdoors at heart, my family's demands were constricting and suffocating. The west offered an escape, mainly because the wide open mountain ranges gave me the false impression that I'd be free to do anything I wanted without answering to anyone.

I had to go, at least for a visit, to find out if my dream held any substance. My trip plan, which I had drawn up long before I ever got to go, would take me from Minnesota through South Dakota to Montana, south through Idaho, Wyoming and Utah to Arizona, and back again via Nevada, Utah, Colorado and Nebraska. I'd visit stunning national parks of Glacier, Yellowstone, Arches, Grand Canyon, Zion, and Bryce Canyon. I would even visit the Hoover Dam, and the famous Colorado ski resort cities of Aspen, and Vail in addition to many other less famous stops. I researched my planned stops and marked the maps and drew up to-do lists. Most importantly, I even started putting money aside for the trip instead of just talking the talk about doing so.

It seemed like every waking moment was spent polishing my plan with my anticipation of being on the open road providing the high I normally bought with the money I was putting aside. I explained the details of my trip to whomever would listen, mostly out of pride, but also because I'd hoped that someone would be persuaded to join me.

As excited as I was to be going, part of me didn't want to do it alone. A long trip such as that would be better with someone to share it with, and I knew that. However, my loner side jealously wanted to do the trip alone. Many people scoffed at the idea of me actually pulling it off; a factor that fueled my desire and motivated me to show them.

A year after high school, I finally had enough cash to go west. I filled my car with all the camping and cooking supplies I would need for a journey of a couple thousand miles and almost ten states. I made sure I had my hiking gear, since a big part of my plan revolved around hiking to see the sights most tourists missed. Next I packed what I thought was enough food and water for a two week trip into a cooler with a large block of ice to keep it fresh. In addition to my stash of money, I loaded another stash - my marijuana, pipe, lighter, and matches. By the time I finished loading all the items on my lists, my small red sports car was packed to the brim.

When the countdown to departure arrived, I jumped in, turned on the ignition, smiled like a child on Christmas morning, shifted into reverse and maneuvered down the driveway.

I waved goodbye to my teary-eyed mother as I backed up. As she stood there watching her only son drive away into the sunset, her eyes held a concern that I perceived as something negative. It was only later in life that I understood that concerned look involved my well-being and safety.

My parents had asked me multiple times to think again about what I was doing, and to make sure I wasn't making a rash decision. I thought they were trying to dominate and intimidate me. I hadn't realized they were more scared for me than I was for myself of the great unknown in front of me. I was young, brash, and full of confidence in myself. I was too stubborn to be dissuaded from making my dream trip.

My solo trip was to commence. I lit my marijuana pipe and turned up my favorite music as I passed the small town city limits sign and headed down the highway. There was nothing but open road ahead of me. The joy I felt as I departed from my neighborhood, town, and the state of Minnesota was overwhelming. I sang out at the top of my lungs with the radio, and all my treasured music I brought on CD's and cassette tapes.

One hand held an atlas while the other gripped the steering wheel. Behind me were the rules, constraints, and nagging, and in front of me, at long last, lay freedom. I was able to cruise down the road and go anywhere I wanted, and no one would question my choice.

All those years of hoping and bragging, months of planning and anticipating were coming true. What to do? Where to go? The possibilities were almost endless.

I knew exactly where to land on the first part of my journey. Years before, some friends, my track coach, and I had taken a short camping trip west, to the Badlands in South Dakota. A return to old memories would be like a gateway to new ones. Actually seeing the Badlands on my own would be much more rewarding than just having a quick camp and drive by photo shoot to prove I had been there as had happened previously.

When I completed the almost five hundred mile drive to my first destination, I found out how welcoming the Badlands were to a traveler who had driven what felt like an eternity on flat, boring, prairie land. One advantage with the flatness was that I could see off in the distance and behold the tall jagged spires, which as I drew closer, collapsed into massive eroding buttes. Those rough nature-sculpted rocks beckoned to me like a string of lighthouses on the edge of a prairie ocean as I drove down Interstate 90 through South Dakota.

As I prepared to bed down for my first night away from home, it felt like a huge chapter of my life had just come to a close. I now felt as if my life was my own and not someone else's.

The next morning as I gathered my belongings and rolled up my tent to continue my adventure of a lifetime, the wild thought dominating my mind was that no one knew where I was. I liked it.

Reality set in a bit when I was camped up near Glacier National Park in northern Montana. Still new to being on the road solo, I picked a campsite and set up my spot with my tent, campfire and cooking stove. Just as I was going to settle down to a little steak, beans and potato dinner, a camper walked up.

"Hello, fellow camper."

"Hi there," I replied, startled a bit.

"Don't mean to intrude during your dinner, but wanted to let you know a bear was spotted here not but an hour or two ago."

"A bear?" My response revealed a hint of excitement in my voice.

"Yes, a bear, so be careful please. It's a beautiful night out tonight. A little cool out, but expected this early time of year. Bears are just starting to wake up and move around looking for food. Wonderful night nonetheless. My family and I are camping on the other side of the park if you should need anything, just let us know. Enjoy."

"Thank you, I will. You too, sir."

In retrospect I'm thankful I never saw that bear the camper mentioned.

A few days later my solo trip out west brought me to the edge of the Grand Canyon via a less traveled gravel road that led out to a loop. I parked and stepped out of my car. Nobody was around and no vehicles were in sight. The only sign of others in the area came from a light in the far distance. I was alone and sat on the edge of the canyon overlooking the Colorado River over a mile below. It was a remarkably breathtaking yet brought on an eerie feeling being alone this far away from home not knowing exactly where I was.

Just then I saw dust flying up and a blue color moving in the distance toward me. I got nervous when a rusty old blue pickup truck pulled up beside my fancy red sports car. An older man with tanned leathery skin stepped out and turned to me.

"Nice." The man said in a low soft voice pointing around the canyon.

"Yes."

"Smoke?"

"I'm sorry, what?"

"Smoke? Pipe?" The man asked again in that soft voice. It occurred to me the man only knew enough English to make brief communication. The man was looking for a pipe to use. Keeping an eye on the man, I walked to my car while pondering the man's intentions. I grabbed my pipe, turned and handed it to the man, who stood waiting with his palm up.

"Be back." The man said as he took the pipe and walked to the edge of the canyon. I stood near my car pretending to be busy, while I kept my eyes on the visitor. The man spent a few moments having a smoke break and watching the sunset bounce up the canyon walls providing a light show only God can create. Minutes later the man returned with a big smile. He handed me the pipe and walked to the back of his pickup truck. The man grabbed a small box and filled it with some cardboard trash, small pieces of wood and some pine cones. He turned back to me.

"No tent."

"Excuse me? I don't understand."

"No tent." The man said again, pointing to the light far off in the distance. It then occurred to me that setting up my tent there for the night probably wasn't a good idea. With darkness quickly approaching, the man waved, as he drove away. Curious about what the man smoked in his pipe, I glanced down to find it was filled with dark colored marijuana. I wasted no time in lighting the pipe and smoking the little gift my new friend just left. Soon after, hallucinations set in causing the ground underneath me to seem to move. Alarmed, I was smart enough to know standing near the edge of a steep cliff was not a good thing to do when high like this. I thought it best to get in my car and stay there for the night.

I left the moment the morning sun rays touched my car. I figured I had enough of living on this canyon edge. Passing some twisted spiky Joshua trees, the Hoover Dam, and wild shaped boulder piles, my next target on my map was Zion and Bryce Canyon National Parks.

Each park presented itself with a unique story. Zion with its warm air and multicolored sandstone cliffs gave way to a perfect day hike through the narrow gorges and slot canyons. Bryce Canyon provided a horizon full of odd shaped pillars of rock called Hoodoos. I ran into a group of friendly hikers while camped at Bryce Canyon National Park, who invited me to their campsite for a night long party filled with tequila liquor shots and plenty of high-potent marijuana.

Morning came too quickly as I, extremely hung-over, unzipped my tent to find a fresh blanket of snow. I was worn out from being on the road for two weeks and decided it was time to head back home to Minnesota through Colorado. The stop in Colorado is what developed the urge for my permanent move out west later.

I made sure that people, including myself in future years, would know where I'd been by keeping a travel log of the roads I drove, scenic stops I visited, and campsites where I had spent the night. I took hundreds of pictures that I could show off when I returned home. This trip made a huge impact on my life. I would talk about my solo trip for years to come.

Chapter 11

Stay West Young Man

The trip west itself did not change me, but I came back looking for more out of life than I had before I went. I longed to have more of an identity of who I really was and a vision for a future.

After returning from the long trek, I was fortunate enough to find a job assisting the management in a lumber yard. The only thing in my head however was the trip I had just taken out west. It was constantly on my mind, and thus my concentration on the new job was poor.

The fighting with my sister and mother became more intense at home. I was convinced my pride and arrogance was the major source of our arguments as I tried to dictate to them the best way to run a home. Most of my friends were out of town away at college. Some were already married. Some were still partying and living life in the "fast-lane" doing what they had done in high school - only more so. It just didn't feel right for me to be in Hutchinson any more.

Something clicked in me after only two months on the new job. At work one day, I headed to the lumber warehouse to fulfill a customer's order but paused to sit in one of the large doorways and light up a cigarette. I gazed towards the horizon, thinking of the remarkable time I had on my recent solo trip out West. I suddenly knew it was necessary for me to leave town. I was tired of the fighting, the "old high school ways", and of working a job I felt was never intended for me. It was time to find my destiny.

When the fall of 1995 rolled around, I packed my belongings into a U-Haul truck. The only person I knew out west was an old friend from school who lived in Colorado. I hoped my buddy could get me a few contacts for work or whatever else I would need help finding.

Before I left for greener pastures, I visited my grandmother to apply my soft touch on her heart strings to score a little cash for my trip.

"Grandma, I'm leaving town."

"Where are you going Andy?"

"Colorado."

"What are you going to do out there?" My grandmother asked.

"I think I'm going to go to school. At least I'll look around. Maybe look into becoming a ski patrol. I could use a little money until I find work though."

Grandma said nothing more as she graciously went to her purse and pulled out her checkbook. A couple of minutes later, after a brief hug and quick exchange of words, I walked out with the check folded up in placed it in my wallet. I had not even looked at it in hopes it was at least a few hundred dollars.

After pulling my car onto the trailer that would be pulled behind the U-Haul, I said goodbye to my mom and jumped into the truck. Hardly looking back at my mother, standing in the driveway and wiping the tears with one hand and waving goodbye to me with the other, I engaged the transmission on the U-Haul and pulled away. I was free again.

Before hitting the open road, I stopped at my adopted brother's apartment to show him and friends I

was packed and serious about my move out west. We
smoked a little dope and celebrated one last time. It
was an odd feeling not knowing when I would see
anyone again. I didn't linger there long though because
my dream was calling me. I was ready to get high and
play in the mountains again.

Driving down the interstate with everything I
owned in the U-Haul and my car on a trailer behind me
made me very nervous. Thoughts were bouncing
through my mind with every mile. One mile I was
excited, and the next I was scared to death. In fact
each mile seemed to provoke its own unique feeling.

There was no job or even known job prospects
waiting for me. I had no place to live. Maybe I had
bitten off more than I'd be able to chew and digest.
What I did have was almost nine hundred miles of
highway in front of me and just myself to talk to.

It was then that I remembered the check my
grandmother had given me. In my haste to escape, I
hadn't even bothered to look at the amount written on
that little piece of paper. I hoped it was at least a
couple hundred dollars. I reached into my wallet and
pulled the check out. When I saw the number of
zeroes on the check, I almost lost control of the U-Haul.
My grandmother had gifted me with ten thousand
dollars. I screamed with excitement.

I pulled off the highway to a rest stop and called my friend in Colorado. "Party's on me, man!" I'm buying, so get ready to party!

I filled and lit my pipe again. I smoked more pot on the drive to Denver, Colorado than I ever had before.

At eleven at night, I pulled into Denver. I had no clue where I was going, and almost drove right through the metropolitan city. I called my one friend in the area twice to receive more detailed directions to his place, where I would sleep for the evening.

The second night I had an urge to "tear up the town." My friend had to work, so I decided to explore the big city alone. I was unemployed, so it didn't really matter how late I stayed out. With a small map of downtown Denver in hand, I located a club downtown and ventured out into the urban traffic. I never found that specific club. However, I found a few others. Driving around a big city with a population of more than two million after living in a town with fifteen thousand citizens was extremely overwhelming. Trying to find my way back to where I was staying would have been incredibly frightening if I had been sober. I wasn't, making it a minor miracle I got home that night.

I roomed with my friend for a month in Golden, Colorado but moved into my own place after things went sour with my buddy. The good little boy from Minnesota seemed lost. I had burned up almost half of the ten thousand dollars I started my Denver adventure with on clubs, alcohol, weed, cocaine, and "crank" (crystal methamphetamine). After two months of being unemployed and burning money like there was an endless supply, I realized the "fun" had to slow down. The last thing I wanted was to crawl back home a loser needing my mommy and daddy to support me again. This was my time, my start and my new journey in life. With all my heart, I wanted to make a life for myself on my own. I vowed that I would never move back to Hutchinson, Minnesota, and I meant to keep that vow.

I started school the beginning of 1996, partly to help myself slowdown from the party life and excessive spending. I realized very quickly I could gain a little extra cash from my family back home because I was working towards a college degree. I also accepted a physically demanding job loading semi-trailers with people's packages at a packaging factory. When that job fell through, I landed a construction clean-up job ensuring the construction site was in order. This led to me moving up to be an apprentice, steel stud framing the new construction.

My drug and party life didn't slow down enough as even that job ended shorter than expected. I dug in and soon accepted a job professionally cleaning homes and businesses. Going in to clean up after others was not my ideal career choice. But, I was willing to take any job if it meant paying the bills to show family and friends back home I could make it on my own. My crazy lifestyle slowed down but never came to a complete stop.

I met a girl named Hope (not her real name) on a ski trip in Aspen that winter while my uncle was visiting. I witnessed Hope in a bar being angrily confronted by her own father. Since I was in need of a roommate and she appeared to need help, I asked Hope if she would like to move in with me. I figured it was better for both of us since we both were basically on our own and not doing well financially. Two months later, she did just that.

In the next chapter of my life, I spent most of my free time with Hope. We drove around in the mountains and smoked marijuana together almost every day. The mountains had a tranquilizing effect on both of us and seemed to make all the worries of the world disappear - until we drove back toward town.

I switched my major in college from Computer Engineering to Park Ranger. I was not fond of sitting for long periods of time, and I loved being outdoors, so this switch was a perfect fit.

With the new major, I was fortunate enough to land a job with the Colorado State Parks working as a dispatch/gate attendant for Chatfield State Park. That park was located twenty miles southwest of Denver near the mountains. I loved that side of Denver close to the mountains, and finding a job that close to home was a stroke of luck. My new stream of income not only covered the food and rent on the apartment I needed, but also helped fund my party habit.

The Chatfield State Park job fortunately opened another door for me. With the help and favor of fellow rangers, I found employment with the City of Lakewood at Bear Creek Lake Park in the same general geographic location. This time however, I was in no way a desk jockey. I landed an actual park ranger position, a job that I immediately loved doing. It not only taught me more than I ever knew about the outdoors, but it taught me responsibility. It was by far the most important (and lucrative) achievement concerning my career so far. I was forging out a new life of my own, and it was good.

My memories of finding Roxborough State Park and falling in love with the park's solitude, scenery and wildlife ended the stream of life events that had continuously paraded through my mind. That love I'd developed for the trail had brought me to the place where I was right now - deadlocked in the jaws of a Puma (Felis) Concolor, better known as a mountain lion, cougar or panther. In the blink of an eye, I was snapped back to reality.

Chapter 12

Meanwhile, Back at the Mountain

I screamed, "GOD! Please help me! I don't want to die! Not here. Not now. Not like this. HELP! GOD! Please help me! I'll do anything! I just don't wanna die!"

I didn't know if God heard me or even wanted to hear me, but it was apparent that God was my only hope.

"I have things I want to do. I'm sorry God! Please! I want to be remembered better. God, please save me! I need you now!"

As I desperately yelled out my prayer as loudly as I could, I heard the lion's fangs crunch down one more time, again raking against my skull. The blood flowed freely now down onto my face like a faucet, and I knew the blood was mine and not the cats. I hadn't even put a scratch on the lion's face or head as far as I could tell.

I yelled out to anyone within hearing distance, "Help! Lion! Please help me! I'm not ready to die, not like this! God please help me!"

My life that had flashed through my mind had not impressed me at all. I didn't want anyone to read about Andy Peterson and the life I lived to this point in time. That was not the legacy I had hoped to leave behind when my time came.

It was perhaps too late for my understanding of the concept of choices, but for some reason the thought struck me that we all are given the ability to make choices in life, both good and bad. And that those choices have consequences. And it suddenly dawned on me that most of my choices had been bad ones leading up to this point in time. And those bad, selfish choices had hurt a good number of people. I had done whatever needed to be done to get a head in life thus far. Proverbially stabbing friends and family in the back and not really thinking twice about it. Here I was almost three miles into the mountains, with my head literally in the jaws of a mountain lion that was on the verge of having me for dinner. If only I had made better choices when I was young, I wouldn't be in this predicament of fighting for my life. These were the thoughts flying through my mind as the curtain seemed to be descending on my life.

I thought about my party friends and the fact that none of them were there to help me. How would I be remembered? Would they mourn the loss of a funny guy? Or mourn the legacy of a party guy? Or perhaps even a nice guy? What difference did it make? At twenty-four years old, I was too young to have my life snuffed out. I had escaped from a number of problems during my young life through my manipulative means. There was no way I would fool the cougar into giving me what I wanted. Here, locked in the animal's incredibly powerful mouth and razor sharp claws, I'd discovered a reality that I couldn't deny or avoid.

I decided to fight back with all I had inside me.

On my knees with my head locked in the lion's jaws, I could see the teeth and look right down the lion's mouth. The stench of death was incredibly strong as I felt myself being scalped alive. I remembered I had the knife clenched in my left hand and tried to penetrate the lion's neck with its small blade. I saw fur fly as I desperately continued to stab the cougar's neck, but there was no evidence of bleeding from the lion.

Every time I made contact with the knife, the blade squeezed down on my finger, cutting into my own bone because there was no lock. As a last, desperate move, I reached over the cat's head with my right hand and felt two soft bumps. I jabbed my right thumb into one soft spot, which turned out to be the right eye of the beast, as hard as I could, digging past the eyelid and around the eye itself. The lion let out a wicked squeal.

I changed my target to the top of the head and swung my left hand, fiercely gripping the knife, down with all the strength I could muster up as I yelled at the cat, "Let go of me!"

The claws in my neck loosened up and at that moment I heard popping noises again as the claws came out. The jaws also loosened as the lion let out a baby-like chirp. I didn't hesitate, but pulled my head back out of the jaws of death. The mountain lion took two swipes at my face and gashed me under my left eye, giving way to a loud popping sound as the claw tore the skin wide open. I didn't wait around for more as I jumped up on the trail and stood looking down on the lion ten feet below on the mountain side. Blood stained the right side of the animal. Although, I knew most of the blood was my own. The cat's right eye was mushy and gray in color.

I was pretty sure the cougar had plenty more fight in him, so I needed to offer up more proof that tearing me open and eating me would be more trouble that it was worth. With my left hand still deadlocked around the knife bleeding, I reached down with my right hand and grabbed baseball sized rocks and hurled them toward the beast as fast and hard as I could. None of them hit my target. It might have helped if I could have used my left hand, since I was left handed. I turned in desperation and saw a basketball sized rock halfway stuck in the dirt off the trail near my left foot. I reached with both hands and ripped it out of the ground and raised it above my head before flinging it through the air with all my might. This time the large rock slammed straight into the cat's side, forcing the lion about three more feet down the side of the mountain.

At that point, I figured it was time to beat a hasty retreat, if the lion would let me go. I figured it was about thirty minutes since I had first spotted the cat. I had been locked into the fight for my life for at least fifteen minutes. I started sprinting down the trail, gravity helping pull me along despite my fatigue and loss of blood. There was still nobody in sight.

Running down the mountain, I wondered how badly I was hurt. I wondered how bad my neck was ripped open or my head chewed up. I hoped that the lion was not chasing me as I kept glancing back over my shoulder praying the animal was not closing in. There was no way I could outrun a mountain lion, and now I was exposing my backside as I almost flew down the steep winding trail. There were still a few snow drifts along the trail and not knowing how bad my wounds were, I grabbed the white snow and slapped it up on my mangled head. I watched in horror as the snow quickly fell back to the ground, splattering the pristine snow with crimson. I continued to cast a look over my shoulder now and again to see if I was being followed. Thankfully, there was no sign of the killer.

I couldn't drink from my water bottle since I couldn't swallow and wasn't about to stop running to take a drink anyway. I raced another mile and a half down the mountain scared to death the lion was gaining on me. In the last mile there was a huge stand of ponderosa pine trees near where the trail featured an L shaped configuration. Blazing down the trail around the L shaped corner, I looked once again over my right shoulder only to see the mountain lion glaring at me in attack position off the trail right at the corner of the stand of Ponderosa pines.

You gotta be kiddin' me. Please. No more.

I turned and took two more steps down the trail. I looked back in fear expecting to see the lion launching at me in midair. There was no lion on the trail. And there was no trace of a lion in that spot where the beast had previously been. Instead of the body of a cougar, I saw a bearded transparent face.

I stopped running. "Jesus?" Years later, as a guest on the Oprah Winfrey Show, Oprah asked me how I knew it was the face of Jesus. I replied, "Well, it wasn't the ice cream man!" The moment I saw His face, an incredible overwhelming peace rushed over me, and I felt convinced that this was the face of a man I needed to know. I suddenly felt as if nothing could touch me because I was in the hands of a protector. An inaudible voice went through my head.

"I got ya, son, I got ya. Do you want a second chance in life? If you want a second chance, show me. Get down this mountain and start living for me. I got this. Go and start living for me, and I'll give you that second chance."

I took off running again, looking down at my legs as I went. My legs were running so fast around the steep switch-backs descending down the trail that I had trouble controlling them. I knew I now had help getting down that mountain. The thick tall stand of ponderosa pine trees opened up to give way to the trail below. People! I saw actual people! "Help me! Help! 911! Call 911! Lion! I screamed with all the energy I had left.

I quickly gained ground and came upon the couple on the trail. They stopped there as I ran right into their arms. I was so happy to finally see people. I was convinced my skull was showing, and my eyes were still dripping blood, a frightening sight I'm sure. The surprised couple helped to sit me down on the uphill side of the trail.

"Sit down and rest. You need to drink something," the man said.

I can't. God told me I have to get down this mountain.

"I gotta keep going. He said to keep running."

I pulled away from them and took off again down the mountain as the couple stared helplessly at my retreating figure.

Unknown to myself, the four ladies I had ungraciously passed earlier in my climb were just driving away as I screamed for help. Miraculously, they heard my frantic cries for assistance, turned around, parked their car, and hurried back up the trail to assist me. I, not wanting to stop knowing my instructions for a second chance in life came directly from God, ran right past the four ladies. I reached the maintenance access road which was half a mile from the start of trail and visitors' center. I calculated that I had traveled about two and a half miles in about fifteen minutes. My track coach would have been proud of me. Breathless now, I had nothing left.

Another lone female hiker appeared. Her eyes got huge when she saw me and the condition I was in.

"Help me! 911! Lion! Lion!" I croaked.

She turned and took off running.

Why is she running away from me? Is she going to call for help?

I was now having difficulty breathing after fighting for my life against a razor sharp killing machine and running desperately almost three miles down a steep mountain. I started staggering down the trail one step at a time bound and determined to get down that mountain. I was not going to give up now. Not after fighting this hard. Not after what God told me to get my life back again. All of a sudden each of my arms went up over a pair of shoulders, and the four ladies I had almost ignored earlier assisted me. Holding me upright, we continued down the trail as they basically carried me the last half mile to the visitors' center, my feet dragging along the dirt path below.

They encouraged me. "You're doing great! You're doing great! Hang in there. We're almost there."

I thought I was in trouble because I was not doing it by myself and that's what I believed God told me to do. I was in no condition to protest however and try to make it on my own. I was so very thankful for those ladies and their help.

They managed to get me, a severely injured man to the visitors' center. For the first time since I had escaped the lion, I suddenly felt agonizing pain. Pain shot through my entire body. My feet felt as though they were on fire and going to explode. One lady removed my bloody shoes and massaged my feet. Another dampened my head and face with a cool wet rag.

"You're doing great! You're doing great! Rescue is almost here."

I didn't feel so great. The pulsating whirring of helicopter blades drew my attention and became louder as a rescue chopper drew closer.

A few minutes later, a sudden rush of pain came over me as I was receiving I.V.'s from the Flight for Life crew. As soon as the rescuers had me stabilized and secured to a gurney, I was wheeled outside towards the helicopter. The warmth and brightness of the sun was a welcomed relief for me as I knew then I made it down that mountain doing what God had asked. I found the flight itself to be surreal as I watched the black visors of the rescuer's helmets as they maneuvered the chopper through the Colorado skies.

I analyzed my current condition. *What a sight I must have been. My forehead ripped apart and hanging down to reveal my skull. My eye and face gashed open. The top of my head and neck chewed up and punctured from the lion's teeth and claws. My legs, arms, and chest the same. And my hands covered in globs of blood and fur. I am a mangled mess.*

Eight minutes later, I arrived at the Swedish Medical Center and was quickly wheeled into the emergency room. The emergency room was quiet as the nurses and doctors tried to evaluate my condition after the rare mountain lion encounter. I could hear the phone calls being made to my family back in Minnesota. I was comforted to know that my family was immediately on their way to see me.

I made it! Wow! What will mom and dad think now?

I was resting on the hospital bed as the emergency crew worked around me finally putting me under anesthesia.

My last thought being, *I'd been saved!*

Chapter 13

Math and Aftermath

The doctors discovered I had bite marks that totaled two feet in length all around my skull. Six hours of surgery followed my arrival to repair the damage wreaked by the powerful cougar. I required plastic surgery on my face where the lion had raked a four inch gash one millimeter away from and under my left eye. Because of the wounds in my scalp, the doctors couldn't shave my head before stapling the bite marks closed or the roots of hair would have came out. I lost only one percent of my hair with the remarkable patch work of the surgeon. Seventy staples (two staple guns) were needed to close the wounds on my head. The surgeon had never even used two staple guns on the same patient before in his twenty years of emergency medical work. I received approximately one hundred stitches in my neck, chest, stomach and legs closing bite and puncture wounds. Ironically, although I was anemic, I didn't require blood transfusions due to the dry Colorado air that frightful day quickly drying most of the wounds.

After surgery, I attempted to sleep, but approximately every twenty minutes or so, I relived my nightmarish mountain lion attack over and over again in my head. All night long, I would scream out with these night terrors and with little success attempt to jump up to get away, sweating and trembling with fear. My mind was replaying the cougar attack over and over again preventing me from getting some crucial doctor recommended sleep.

My family members began arriving at my bed side. My father, whom I considered a Jesus freak and whom I laughed at for having weird beliefs, was the last to enter my room.

"I need to ask everyone to please step out of the room as I'd like to talk to Andy - just father and son."

Everyone complied with the request, so I found myself a captive audience with my dad, the Jesus freak.

"Yeah, you got scars like the old man. It's about time. How you doing in here? My dad asked, pointing to his heart.

Huh?" I had no clue how to answer that question.

"Can I tell you about my best friend, Jesus?"

"I'm not going anywhere. I mean...I guess so."

For the next hour, my dad poured out his heart to me about the goodness of Jesus. How he had peace in the morning. Peace at night and a peace unlike anything else he had ever felt before in his life.

"I've realized I don't have control of everything. God has it all under control. Son, Jesus is my best friend. I've learned one thing, that if I try to control what's happening around me, I tend to mess it up. That's the reason I've given everything to the Lord."

After the vision on the mountain and my miraculous escape, I didn't see any way that I could refuse the invitation my father extended for me to accept Jesus as my Savior. I recited the sinner's prayer there in my hospital bed asking Jesus into my heart, to forgive me of every one of my past sins, and to give me the courage and strength to trust Him so I could start living for the Lord.

As I reflected back on it later, at that point, I truthfully only put one foot of mine on God's path, a fact little known to my father.

My hospital stay was quite an experience in itself. Two wonderful traveling nurses stopped by regularly in the first part of my stay to ensure that their patient was doing well. If I needed morphine for the excruciating pain, relief was just a button push away.

That luxury didn't last as my condition improved. Morphine was later administered by nurses after evaluating pain levels.

According to one of the nurses, my room became a refuge for nurses escaping from less than pleasant patients and duties. I didn't complain at all as nurses dropped by my room throughout the day simply to say hello and take a breather from their normal stressful overworked routines. The room across the hall housed an older gentleman who was incredibly disrespectful, so the nurses found it refreshing to stop over and get a few laughs and conversation with me, the charming mangled park ranger. Their presence gave me a chance to flirt a little as well, even though I wasn't exactly at my best. That pleasurable activity helped me cope with the other, less than enjoyable, aspects of being injured and being in a hospital. Over the four days in the hospital, I made it a habit to wheel my I.V. pole down the hallway to wave and smile at as many other patients as I could. I made sure to give them a sincere hello. My little walk a few times a day became a refreshing highlight for many others as well as accelerating healing for myself.

The park rangers kept me updated of their search for the mountain lion that had attacked me. Success in trapping the lion would determine if I had to undergo rabies shots or not. If the division of wildlife trapped it, tests would determine if the animal was rabid. A positive test would be negative for me. If they didn't find and test the animal within three days, the worst would have to be assumed.

A team with the division of wildlife brought in search hounds and tracked the animal unsuccessfully for three days. Each location the hounds led the team to in the mountains concluded with a similar blood spotted area below a tree of flattened leaves and brush. The three day limit expired without any lion being captured.

I braced myself as a handful of nurses entered my room. Two female nurses stood on my left with a dozen large syringes.

A male nurse on my right reached out his hand and said, "Squeeze my hand - you're going to need it."

I wasn't exactly thrilled at the prospect of holding hands with a male nurse, especially when there was some of the female variety available, but I obeyed. Twelve intensely painful shots on the top of my head deep into the bite marks and several screams later, I had to get assistance to undo my fingers which were locked around the nurse's hand. My hand was so numb I couldn't even feel it so I could release my death grip on the poor guy who was trying to help me survive the mind boggling pain.

The next day the male nurse bravely walked into my room to say hello and check on me. He was wearing a cast around his last two fingers. I had unknowingly broken them. I felt bad as the nurse related that it was the first time anyone had ever broken his fingers holding hands with him.

The nurse joked about it and we both had a good laugh. I relayed my gratitude for his help through the excruciating ordeal.

My doctor knew who miraculously saved and healed his patient. He asked if he could use me as a test subject and apologized for not taking more pictures of me when I first arrived at the hospital by Flight for

Life. He mentioned it looked like I had a red mask on with my forehead hanging down to reveal my skull.

"You were quite a sight, my friend. A lot of people were a little shaken up by the whole thing." I sat and listened with a thankful heart.

Four days after I had been airlifted in, I was officially released and assisted by wheelchair as standard procedure out of the hospital. As the nurse wheeled me out of the hospital and into the bright warm Denver air, my lion encounter and brush with death seemed surreal. The world somehow seemed different to me. All the trees seemed a bit greener, and the sky appeared a vivid clear blue in color. Everything was moving too fast. From the quiet healing moments in the hospital to the now busy highways of Denver, my life was certainly different. The healing and adjustment to real life again would surely take time.

A ham sandwich never tasted as good as the day I was back at home after miraculously surviving my mountain lion attack. There was no comparison with a home cooked meal versus unflavored hospital food. What I wasn't prepared for was the vivid dreams I was about to have during my sleep. The first night home, exhausted, I went to my room to try and sleep. Within an hour of dosing off, I flew up from the bed out of breath similar to the first dreadful night in the hospital. I was reliving the attack over and over again. With a shortness of breath, I wholeheartedly prayed for the full armor of God.

The next night my dream placed me in a parking lot on the north side of town. It was a drug deal of some sort in the middle of the night. The drug dealer, filled with rage, turned and started walking rapidly towards me. Quickly closing the gap, the drug dealer raised his right fist to take the first punch. I reached down to grab my knife in defense only to have a peace suddenly come over me. I knew this peace. God told me not to worry as He will protect His children. As the drug dealer swung, I braced for a fist to the face only to feel nothing but complete peace. My next vision in the dream, I was resting, engulfed in peace, up against the side of a huge lion. Feeling as though this lion was in complete control and nothing could harm me. I sat up in bed, smiled and knew God's love and peace was unconditional and very much real.

Another dream I had shortly after returning home from the hospital included a stranger, a jeep, and two huge Bengal tigers. Pulling up on the left side of a gas station I noticed a hideous sight. There at the pay phone, on the outside of a gas station, was a man being mauled by two immense tigers. I leaped out of the jeep to help the man in his dire situation by going for the tiger's eyes. Before I could take another step, one of the tigers spoke,

"Go ahead. Try it, boy." Instantly I woke up.

My survival dreams continued with all types, sizes, and colors of lions in the coming days, weeks and months. Each survival dream brought me closer to the Lord to confirm I couldn't live my life without God's grace, love, and protection. I didn't want to. In order to minimize scarring in such a prominent location, I rubbed vitamin E on the cut under my left eye every few hours for a few months after the attack. My surgeon asked me to soak my head in a sink full of warm water for a few minutes at least twice a day to rinse. I wasn't able to wash or scrub my head as the roots of my hair would fall out due to the almost two feet of wounds on the top of my head.

I wore a bandana over my head and looked like a rough unshaven convict as I walked into a restaurant to eat out for the first time since the attack. I stood in line after getting word from the hostess that a wait for our table would be about thirty minutes. I sat with medical steri-strips adhered under my left eye and on my neck to cover the claw puncture wounds. After about five minutes, I had to get out of there. It felt as if everything was closing in on me, causing a panic attack. At that point, I was still trying to comprehend the attack and put the pieces of my life back into place. My home became a safe haven for a few months as I healed.

Unfortunately a week after escaping the hospital, I was smoking marijuana again in the stairwell of my apartment building in Denver, Colorado. I'd made a promise to Jesus, but old habits die hard, and I went right back into the life style that had made me ashamed as the events of my life streamed by during that fateful attack. Some would have accused me of being a dog that returned to its own vomit as scripture alludes to. Now that the immediate danger to my existence was removed, it was easy to slip back into old behavioral patterns. The dreams of terror still haunted me at night, causing me to relive the ordeal, but didn't convince me to lift the other foot out of the world and plant it on God's path. I had put one there, but selfishly I kept the other foot on a more self serving worldly path.

My life was changing slowly around me. My relationship with Hope ended as we were both now on different paths. I was attempting to run on God's path and she was still running down another. I knew I had to move on.

I went back to school in Colorado in a feeble pursuit to finish my degree. I sat in each class trying to focus on the teachers as they went on with their lectures and lessons. However, I sat looking over each person in the class with a strong desire to share one thing and one thing only, my encounter with the mountain lion and my acceptance of the Lord.

I returned to duty as a park ranger a short time later. In early January of 1999, a gentleman who worked for the state overseeing the water in the area stopped by the park where I worked as a ranger. The man lived in a house about fifteen miles into the mountains on a ridge where there were only four other homes. He got my attention quickly.

"Hey Andy, I heard about your amazing story. Incredible you survived, going through an ordeal such as that. I can't imagine the fear you must have felt. The strength of those animals is amazing. Yesterday I spotted a lion with a deer kill on the backside of the ridge."

A chill went up my spine. *Could this be the lion that attacked me?* "I would love to see it. May I come over tomorrow? Will you show me where you saw it?"

"Absolutely, I wasn't sure if you wanted to go look or not. Why don't we ride up together since I know exactly where the lion is with its deer kill?"

"I would love to, thank you!"

I drove into the mountains to pick the man up in the state park's patrol truck the next afternoon. The man lived in the fifth house along the ridge. Once on the ridge, I canvassed the terrain, intensely looking for any possible signs or movements of a lion. I parked as close to the man's front door as possible and ran up to the door, not knowing where the cougar was at that moment.

With both of us back in the truck, we drove out to the sightings area. As we neared that location, my skin started crawling with the hair on the back of my neck standing tall and chills racing all through my body with the rush of adrenaline. I had no idea where the lion was located except that it had been behind a tree on the back side of the ridge somewhere.

We exited the vehicle and lined up side by side as if in military ranks. My eyes darted all around in a frantic attempt to spot the lion.

The other man yelled loudly. "There it is!" There it is!"

I couldn't locate it. I could feel my eyes growing wider as the fear and chills again raced throughout my body. I had no idea where the lion was located. Below the big pine tree tucked in the shadows of the ridge, two eyes protruded through and locked on with mine in yet another stare off. It felt like déjà vu all over again.

Forcing me to keep my eyes locked on the menacing eyes of the killer, I waited for the lion to charge. In a flash, the lion took a giant leap half way down the mountain side away from us. One more remarkable leap allowed the lion to vanish completely down the side of the mountain and into the forest. I stood speechless in amazement and relieved those astounding bounds had been away from me and not towards me.

Later that month, I received a phone call waking me from a deep sleep in the early morning hours. At first I couldn't identify or understand the caller. I soon determined it was a fellow park ranger talking with such excitement that he was impossible to understand. I finally got him to slow down and repeat his message.

A report had come in from the south side of Green Mountain, located on the west side of Denver along the foothills and red rocks, of a lion resting in a tree in a homeowner's backyard. When the owner had let his dogs out that morning at sunrise, they had gone crazy with barking.

So with the wake up phone call now understood, I sprung out of bed like a child at Christmas morning and dressed so quickly that I was still buckling my pants as I ran down the apartment steps towards my car. I hoped none of my neighbors had seen me. Squealing out of the parking lot, I raced down the street towards the location where the lion was supposedly treed. My fellow ranger was filled with anticipation to see if this was the same cougar that had attacked me.

When I arrived at the house, I encountered police vehicles, division of wildlife vehicles, and ranger vehicles as well as a number of others. The house was packed full of people. Everyone in the house knew who I was and about the battle I had waged with a lion, perhaps this very lion. Everyone stepped back giving me a clear path as I walked straight towards the back door of the house leading out to the deck. I glanced up and immediately recognized the markings of black lines above and below the eyes, the same brown and dark brown shades on its head.

As I starred in awe at this amazing animal with full respect, I was asked by many, "Is it the one? Is this the lion that attacked you?"

I said nothing but stood and stared. The lion was now in our territory. I don't and never did blame the lion for attacking me. After all, it was me that was in its backyard in the mountains in the lion's territory. I felt sorry for it, knowing it was simply trying to survive. I didn't want them to kill the lion on my behalf. Because of the news media still wanting my true full detailed story, I knew I had a little power on my side to make anyone look bad if they killed it. For the safety of everyone around, including the lion itself, a division of wildlife officer leaned out the door with a tranquilizer gun and fired two darts into the lion, as this made a way to remove the cat safely from the homeowner's yard.

After a few minutes, a handful of people, myself included, walked out and opened up a tarp below to try to catch the lion. As the tranquilizer medicine started taking effect, the lion began to slip down the tree bark raking its claws along the trees desperately trying to hold on. With a sudden flip it was now free falling with arms and claws stretched out fully aimed straight towards me. I jumped back with a sudden triggered memory of the attack months prior and tumbled over a grill on the edge of the owner's deck to the ground a couple feet below. I was shaken, but unhurt.

A glue-like substance was placed on the lion's eyes as a precaution. If the lion was to wake up from the tranquilizer medicine, it would not be able to open its eyes and launch towards someone. The glue-like substance would wear off soon enough. I walked up near the lion as again everyone moved away enough to make a little path. I leaned down on one knee and humbly brushed my hand along the lion's side. I could feel every muscle along this stunning animal. What a magnificent powerful machine it was. A machine made to kill, pure muscle and beautiful markings. It was a rare moment I cherish to this day. The 110 lb. female lion lay with a broken, but now healed paw, a one inch scar on the top of its head, and its right eye missing.

I stood up and walked back into the house and confronted the division of wildlife officers.

"Are you going to let it go?" I asked.

No one answered.

"Hello, either you release the lion, or I'll make a case against you. Don't kill it on my account."

One of the officers nodded. "We need to perform a couple of tests first, Andy. Then hopefully we can release it. How's that?"

I smiled. "Fair enough. If you do have to kill it, I want to know and I want one tooth." I turned and walked back out of the house to return home.

Four hours later, the lion that almost took my life was released in the mountains forty miles southwest of Denver. She had helped change my life forever. And although she was not aware of it, I had changed hers as well.

Chapter 14

Andy the Angel

About a year after my attack I packed up my belongings and moved back to Minnesota. After my return, my father had gotten me to attend church with him periodically. One day, later that year, at a church service, I told the pastor that I'd participate in Heaven's Gates Hell's Flames as a warrior angel in the drama presentation. People in the church came up and prayed over me that God would bless me as I fulfilled that role.

However, on the night of rehearsals, I visited a local bar and ran into some college buddies.

"Hey, Andy, it's great to see you! You should come with us, man. There's a huge bonfire party at the lake tonight and there will be some beer kegs too. We're going to have a blast. It'll be like old times, man."

"I don't know, guys, not sure I should. I may just hang out here."

"Sure you should. We don't ever get to see you since you've been living out west. You have to come with us."

I resisted for a minute then caved in. "Alright, let's do it."

A short time later I was out at the lake partying just like the old days and on my way to getting as high as a kite. I was cracking the old jokes, sharing old stories, and laughing while others told their crude jokes. A few hours into the party, the night suddenly turned really quiet. I strangely couldn't make conversation with anybody. It was like I didn't even exist. I'd go up and talk to people, and they acted like they didn't even see or hear me. Everything became very awkward.

As I stood near the huge bonfire, it suddenly got very hot, and very deep. Suddenly I heard a crisp, clear, firm voice, "Do you need another cat, son? Do you need another lion?"

I looked around. There was no one around who appeared to have spoken to me. I knew where the voice had come from. The question hit me like a bat to the face. My drug life style and party days stopped cold right then and there. I knew what I had to do to answer the voice. I threw my cigarettes, my beer, and my marijuana joint into the bonfire. I then walked over to the person who had driven me to the party.

"I'm done for tonight. I'll be sitting over by those chairs, so let me know when you head back to town. I'm ready to go home." I sat apart from everybody else the rest of the night trying to figure out this new life of mine.

The next morning, I heard a car horn honking outside my home. I rolled over. *Oh, that's right. I promised Dad I'd go to church. I feel terrible.*

Despite being hung over and feeling like warmed over death, I accompanied my father to church that day. The pastor made an announcement to the congregation that pricked my conscience.

"We still need two warrior angels for the real life scenario play."

Internally I said, "No way", but my hand went up as if someone raised it.

The pastor smiled broadly. "Andy, I believe you raised your hand. Thank you. Now we need one more, anybody else?"

I was in shock. How did my hand go up? In that role, I would have to pray for people. Being a baby Christian and one who wasn't totally dedicated to my walk with the Lord yet, I wasn't ready for that.

The real life drama arrived and the auditorium seats filled. I found myself feeling out of place.

Am I a fake? Should I even be here? Wow, am I nervous. Just go with it. If I back out now what would I tell my dad or pastor?

When the first person approached for prayer that night, I had butterflies. I was no prayer warrior. How would I pray? What could I say? Two ideas came to me. I could always invoke the name of Jesus. The Lord knew what these people wanted and needed better than they did themselves. Jesus knew what battles they were going through. I could just ask for the Lord's love to be poured upon them. It also dawned on me that although these people were not running away in terror from a hungry mountain lion, they were indeed being tracked by a lion who desired to devour them spiritually. My prayer could help bring God's peace to them. The same peace I now know.

That night I figured out that the hardest part of running after Jesus was letting go of my party friends. I had to also let go of my pride as my comfort zone was surely to be tested. My greatest fear was being alone and not having any friends if I completely changed paths in life. I couldn't continue to straddle the fence with one foot in the Godly kingdom and one foot in the worldly one. It was time for me to make the ultimate decision about which foot was going to move. At that point, I lifted my foot out of the world and placed it into the kingdom of God. Peace flooded over me. It was that same peace I felt when I saw the face of Jesus on the mountain running for my life. And that's when I learned that this entire spiritual journey wasn't about a religion, but one hundred percent about a relationship with my best friend, Lord and Savior, Jesus Christ.

I knew that I had to stand on the solid rock of the Lord's because everything else is slippery sand. I also realized that the battle belonged to the Lord, but that everyone who accepts the Lord has a role to play in the fight. And it was my job to discern the white from the black and the gray. There would be no more sitting on the fence. No more standing on both paths. And I had to make choices in the future based on the principles laid down in the word of God.

I went home and immediately began going through all my personal items. I searched every box I had and tossed out all the old memorabilia that triggered a memory of my old party ways. Anything that reminded me of my pot smoking party days was added to the trash pile. The joy that rushed through me as chill bumps danced on my skin was so strong. That joy continued to grow as I continued to clean out my heart and my life.

I had over five hundred music CDs from my party days that I piled up in a box. I took them to the local music store first thing the next morning. I was eager to jump on God's path and knew all areas of my life had to be cleaned up if I was to fully stand with Jesus.

I walked into the store with the box, laid it on the counter and told the store manager working behind the counter I wished to trade those out for their entire Christian music section. The store manager looked up wide eyed and in shock.

"Sir, do you know how good and rare some of these CDs are?"

"Yes, sir, I do." I replied without hesitation.

"If this is what you want to do, then you go right ahead and help yourself. We will figure out something fair for both of us."

Right then the door opened and two younger boys walked in, glanced my way, and then looked over at the manager before turning back to me.

One of them said, "I know what you're doing. Awesome job! There is no other feeling like it then running after the Lord."

At that moment, God's grace and peace came over me as my comfort zone was reestablished. I realized fully, right then, that Jesus is real. Jesus is alive. And Jesus does answer prayers in His own time.

There is only one true path in life to a peace like none other - God's path. I knew I have been saved from the mountain lion attack, but now I am saved by the blood of Jesus Christ. I have been saved...twice!

1 Corinthians 13:13
And now these three remain: faith, hope and love.
But the greatest of these is love.

Chapter 15

God's Grace

I know some people have been near death and never had the experience of having the events of their life pass through their mind. I was not one of them. Of course not everything that was related in this story went through my mind that day, but I wanted to share all of the details because my story is not just about being mauled by a lion. It is the tale of an emotionally messed up young man whose life took a drastic detour with the help of a cougar.

My life was on cruise control in a dangerous comfort zone in the fast lane. I blamed a lot of people other than myself for all the hurt I caused others and my selfish acts. The day I stared a lion in the eyes was a day I could never imagine. It launched a fear so harsh and consuming I had no choice than to cry out to God. My sins were bad and my transgressions heavy my bridge eventually broke. I hit a wall. My fast lane path came to a crashing halt. I had a choice to make.

God heard my cries for mercy and showed me His son Jesus. The mere vision up on that trail brought on such an overwhelming peace I knew my life would be forever different.

I still get stressed, angry and scared. The wonderful thing now is I know the solid rock foundation of the Lord is under me, picking me up, and giving me hope and strength to carry on each and every day. I strive to share Jesus with others bringing them a hope and a peace in witnessing what only the Lord can do.

God has given me many blessings since becoming a born-again believer in Jesus, putting both feet firmly on His path, and living for Him. I have had the honor of speaking and sharing Jesus with many all over the world. I have been happily married to an incredibly beautiful Christ loving woman for almost thirteen years. I've been blessed with two amazing children (daughter 11 and son 10) both recently baptized in Christ, a parent's most joyful experience.

Life is real and not a game. I no longer take things for granted. I am thankful for my dear family and wonderful friends in my life. Every day brings a new opportunity to witness - take it! The feeling of sharing Jesus with others is so incredibly rewarding.

I don't control everything and that is just fine. God is in control and all He wants is to love and provide me. All I need to do is fully trust and lean on Him with all I am, with my whole heart, and with both feet firmly planted on His path.

A relationship takes time to build on. With prayer things begin. So I pray whatever lion is in your life whether it's a death in the family, an addiction you or a loved one is battling, a stubborn illness or something darker, find the courage to grab onto Jesus with all you have. Never let go. Never give up.

Build your life on the foundation of the Lord. Many will mock you or not understand you. A good number or people however will lift you up, support you and pray with you. Never be ashamed of taking a stand for Jesus. Never be so worried about impressing others you lose focus on God. In God's time, you will see, one day with Jesus is better than any elsewhere. With your new personal relationship with your best friend, Lord and Savior Jesus Christ, you too will enjoy that same peace I found up on the mountain that day.

Thank you for reading my story.

Thank you for trusting Jesus!

God Bless you!

Joshua 24:15
As for me and my household,
We will serve the Lord.

"Be self-controlled and alert, your enemy the devil roams around like a roaring lion looking for someone to devour. Resist him, standing firm in the faith." 1 Peter 5: 8-9

Father God, thank you for loving me. I believe in you. Forgive me of my sins Lord and please give me the strength to turn from those sins. I ask you into my heart and my life so that I may be made new to start living for you. Thank you for allowing your Son, Jesus, to die on the Cross for me Lord. Thank you for that one drop of blood you allowed to be shed for me to give me a second chance in life. Thank you for being my best friend, Lord and Savior Jesus. In your mighty loving name I pray. Amen.

John 14:6
I am the Way, the Truth and the Life. No one comes to the Father except through Me.

Lion King Ministries

**Want a captivating speaker
for your next event?**

**Want a survival story of never giving up
and being saved by God's grace
for your next event?**

Andy's story is one you have to hear! Andy Peterson miraculously survived a terrifying mountain lion attack at Roxborough State Park on April 30, 1998. After surviving the incredible attack, Andy received several dozen stitches to his face, neck, shoulders, chest, stomach, and legs. Andy set a record at Swedish Hospital in Englewood, Colorado by requiring seventy staples to close his head wounds.

This is how Lion King Ministries was founded. This amazing story has been shared on Larry King Live (CNN), Oprah Winfrey Show, Animal Planet, A&E Biography, Versus Channel, New Man Magazine, Reader's Digest, Trinity Broadcasting Network (TBN), Outdoor Life Network and Outdoor Life Magazine. Andy has also shared in numerous churches, conferences, wild game dinners, universities, schools, youth events, businesses and many other outreach events.

This testimony, filled with details before, during, and after the incredible mountain lion attack, will fully captivate and touch your heart. Andy's testimony is filled with a message of excitement, hope and inspiration challenging all who hear. Schedule Andy today to hear the full captivating story!

"Being delivered from death and the jaws of a lion is a gift from God. I would not change it for the world. Jesus is real! Jesus is alive! And Jesus does answer prayers!" Today, Andy is a living witness of the love, grace and forgiveness of his best friend, Lord and Savior Jesus Christ! Andy, his wife and two children make their home in Tennessee.

Andy Peterson, Lion King Ministries
Website: www.lionkingministries.com
Facebook: www.facebook.com/lkministries

RECOMMENDATIONS

"Andy, I give you a lot of credit." Larry King
Larry King
CNN Larry King Live Show

Our students loved Andy's presentation about his encounter with a mountain lion…and, with the living God who pursued him with unmatched intensity! My son said it was, "the best sermon he ever heard!" Andy was professional, yet easy-going…intense, yet relational. His testimony is one that moves you to the edge of your seat, and then out of it altogether as the story unfolds. God's call sometimes does sound like a roar!
Pastor James Gomez
Good Shepherd Lutheran Church

I have known Andy for five years and never knew what powerful and exciting testimony he had. Andy takes the stage with anticipation and excitement but all the while humble as he delivers one of the most intense testimonies I have ever heard. From beginning to end you will sit on the edge if your seat with wonder and excitement at what God was able to do through such a horrible experience. If you struggle with questioning if God can really use you or if God even cares about you, listen to Andy's heart as he shares how God took a strung out kid from knowing about God to being intimate with God. I pray God's blessings on him as he continues to evangelize with his powerful testimony.
Scott Cunningham
Central Baptist Church

Our audience was completely captivated by his theatrical movement and intense story. I strongly recommend Andy as he will most certainly "wow" your audience.
Jeff E. Belts
Hydesville Community Church

The students were encouraged with the message that, in spite of bad circumstances, God has a purpose and plan for each life. As one student wrote in their **yearbook**, "It was the highlight of my school year!"
Noel Cherry
Fellowship of Christian Athletes

"Do you want a story that will grip you? Do you want someone who will share the gospel of Jesus Christ? Andy has an amazing story that speaks to you emotionally, physically and spiritually.
Rich Griffith
Woodmen Valley Chapel

I highly recommend Andy for any group that's considering him for an event. His ability to keep an audience's attention and testimony of what God turned from a seeming tragedy to a life changing encounter will communicate volumes about our Lord's love for us and His passion for a relationship with us all. You will not be disappointed.
Jim Caughey
Fox River Christian Church

It was a privilege to have you on the "Praise the Lord" program in Costa Mesa. Your account of surviving a lion attack was riveting, and your testimony of seeing Jesus' face was powerful!
Paul & Jan Crouch
Trinity Broadcasting Network

You will not be sorry if you invite Andy to your event. His story thrills young and old alike. I highly recommend him!
Mike Dillman
Manteca Christian School

"Thank You," for your heart wrenching and inspirational testimony that you gave at Autumn Acres. Once again, I would like to say Thanks for being such and awesome speaker!!!!
Stephanie Brown Woods
Autumn Acres Corn Maze & Pumpkin Patch

Your story was not only amazing but a true inspiration in what God can do in someone's life. I watched the group smile, wince and even shudder when your story was told. The men were inspired by your faith and courage. We would welcome you back anytime to speak to our congregation and I want to say again, thanks for coming and being a part of our group and sharing your faith and love for Jesus.
Randy Johnson
First Baptist Church

Andy was the keynote speaker at our sportsman's banquet. I know Andy impacted everyone that attended our event as 220 took a stand for Christ!
Jerry Zirk
Riverside Church

I can say without hesitation that his unique presentation style brought his story of survival to life. Listening to Andy's tale, I felt as though I was right there, sharing the experience with him. The incredible odds through which God delivered him makes his ultimate testimony all the more powerful. Truly compelling speakers know how to capture and maintain the attention of their audience, and Andy excels in this. From the youngest children in our congregation to the most senior members, all were engaged in Andy's vivid, energetic presentation. I have now had the opportunity to hear Andy's incredible story on two occasions, and I'd stand in line to do so again.
Patrick Erickson
Pine Grove Church

WOW!!! I just wanted to let you know how much I thoroughly enjoyed your testimony and story at the lunch today - very inspirational and moving. Thank you for sharing your faith and your life experiences.
Marty Gibson
United Methodist Church

Andy's story is so compelling as to spiritually lift the heart of the believer and open the heart of a skeptic.
John Shanks
John Shanks Music

Andy was a fantastic guest on my radio program, telling his story with great enthusiasm and honesty. The nature of his experience is captivating on its own, but Andy brings a life-changing result to the table with humility and passion. I found myself, even as the host of the program, gripping my seat as he talked about the attack. A remarkable individual, with a remarkable event to share, who God is using in remarkable ways to change lives!
Ken Whatmore
Radio 323

Andy Peterson's testimony is dynamic. The transformation that has taken place is nothing less than a miracle. The Lord used a mountain lion to get his attention. His story will grip an audience and cause people to look deep into their heart and find what it is that is holding them back from taking that next step with Christ.
James Rogers
Christ the King Lutheran Church

The best part is your testimonial. It is subtle yet powerful. The Lord drops pebbles, then stones, then rocks, then boulders on your head, (or mountain lions), to get His point across. Please keep this wonderful ministry going. KEEP UP THE GOD WORK!
Dave and Trevor Bohn
Sportsman's Event Planner

It was a pleasure to work with you. Your amazing story is an inspiration to everyone who hears it.
Kevin Fay
Orion Multimedia

Andy's riveting tale of survival and life transformation after being attacked by a Mountain Lion will keep you on edge wanting to know the rest of the story. Our Creator gets Andy's attention using part of His creation, which we may view as beautiful but in this case dangerous and the outcome is life changing. To God be the Glory!!!
Billy Kemp
Central Baptist Church

Andy's story was inspiring and everyone commented on how much they enjoyed his presentation. Andy is passionate about how Christ changed his life. We recommend Andy and know you will be blessed by his story and commitment to Christ.
Oliver Dossmann
Mission to Missionaries

Thanks so much for sharing your testimony at our 50+ Adult Luncheon. What an amazing story! I know that all who attended thoroughly enjoyed your talk. Your presentation was not only exciting but very informative as well.
Scott White
Central Baptist Church

We had the largest crowd ever. We advertised his presentation as an "Edge of Your Seat" story, and indeed it was. But more importantly, his testimony of how God used this experience to change his life was heard by many people that have never set foot inside the door of a Sunday morning service. Praise God!
Garry Wagner
Enterprise First Baptist Church

Andy retold and relived his story that was riveting to both the men and boys alike. Andy shared his love of Christ and the way to the cross. There were definite decisions made for Christ as Andy shared his heart. You will be truly blessed by this amazing, humble young man as he shares his story with your organization.
Rodney & Allyson Johnson
First Baptist Church

To use my 14-year-old daughter's vernacular - he was awesome! Andy encouraged them to walk with Jesus Christ so that the lions crossing their paths will hold no fear for them. Andy gives a powerful, positive, faith-filled, encouraging message for all ages. On behalf of our family in Christ, I encourage your family to hear Andy's story. You will be changed.
Nancy Piper Hovlid
St. John's Lutheran Church
Thank you so much for allowing me to tell your wonderful story. It was truly inspirational.
Shaun Boyd
NEWS4 Colorado

To say the least Andy has a gripping testimony. These normally restless and rambunctious young people sat spellbound as he shared his mountain lion experience and ultimately his experience with the King of Kings. I'd highly recommend Andy. You'll not soon forget his story or the God he pays tribute to.
Bryan Blomkoer
Crow River Area Youth for Christ

I recommend Andy Peterson's ministry without reservation. Andy shared his testimony at our recent Men's Ministry Wild Game Feed. The men were captivated when Andy told the men about the lion that held Andy's head in his mouth! Needless to say, Andy had the men's attention!
Greg Stone
Sunrise Assembly of God

It is my pleasure to give my wholehearted endorsement to the ministry of Andy Peterson and Lion King Ministries. Andy did an amazing job of re-telling his story to a diverse audience while including a clear Gospel presentation. Everyone from the youngest child to the oldest adult present were challenged and encouraged by the message Andy shared. Andy would be an outstanding speaker for your church service or special event.
Len Brisley
Chi Alpha Campus Ministries

How grateful I am for that big cat! The radical changes in Andy's life were set in motion because of that encounter and he will never be the same. It is a tremendous story of the love, grace, and mercy of God that will be a blessing to all who hear. I highly recommend him to you!
Roland Smith
Central Baptist Church

"Dear Andrew, Thank you for being a guest on the show. We appreciate your taking time to share yourself with our viewers and studio audience."
Oprah Winfrey
Oprah Winfrey Show

He gave a very clear, gripping account of his experience with a cougar that had the kids on the edge of their seats. In the end, he clearly presented the gospel and let the kids know that the answer was Jesus to whatever they are searching for in their life. Many of the boys especially commented that they would really listen to the speakers if they were all as good as Andy!! It is hard to reach teen guys and Andy's story is one to grab their attention.
Debbie Fiskum
First Baptist Church

One of my significant memories as a Pastor is when Andy walked through the doors of our church, his first Sunday since being released from the hospital. With stitches and puncture wounds marking his body, he looked like a man who had barely escaped death. Andy was thankful to be alive and ready to begin living a new life. Immediately after the attack Andy's story was sought by various media groups. Andy chose to wait for the Lord's timing to share his dramatic story and the life change, which he has experienced as a result. It seems that now is the time, which the Lord has given the release and the opportunity for Andy to share his testimony. You will find that people identify with Andy and his story. Whether in a men's group, youth gathering or the entire congregation, lives will be touched by this story of survival, new life and reconciliation. I encourage you to consider the testimony of Andy Peterson.

Ken Summers

Teen Challenge & Colorado State Representative

Proverbs 27:19
As water reflects a face,
so a man's heart reflects the man.

PURCHASE ADDITIONAL COPIES

Contact Lion King Ministries today to schedule this must hear inspirational survival story of never giving up and being saved by God's grace for your next event!

Contact Lion King Ministries today to purchase additional copies of *Saved Twice* for your family, friends, co-workers, teachers or simply give as a gift of hope and encouragement to someone!

Andy Peterson, Lion King Ministries
Website: www.lionkingministries.com
Facebook: www.facebook.com/lkministries

Other Sword of the Spirit Publishing Books

2008
All the Voices of the Wind by Donald James Parker
The Bulldog Compact by Donald James Parker
Reforming the Potter's Clay by Donald James Parker
All the Stillness of the Wind by Donald James Parker
All the Fury of the Wind by Donald James Parker
More Than Dust in the Wind by Donald James Parker
Angels of Interstate 29 by Donald James Parker

2009
Love Waits by Donald James Parker
Homeless Like Me by Donald James Parker

2010
Against the Twilight by Donald James Parker
Finding My Heavenly Father by Jeff Reuter

2011
Silver Wind by Donald James Parker
He's So In Love With You by Robert C. Heath
Silver Wind Pow-wow by Donald James Parker
The 21ˢᵗ Century Delusion by Daniel Narvaez
Hush, Little Baby by Deborah M. Piccurelli

2012
The Legacy of Deer Run by Elaine Marie Cooper
Will the Real Christianity Please Stand Up by Donald Parker

2013
The Unexpected Bar Mitzvah by Donald J. Parker
The Accidental Missionary by Rossetti and Parker
The Fleeing Tiara by Dennis Doud
What in God's Name Are We Doing? by Dan McGowan
Knowing Who We Are: Discovering Our True Spiritual Identities in Christ by Mark Calvin Nelson

2014
Right to Believe by Chip Rossetti and Donald.James Parker

Feature Movies from
Sword of the Spirit Publishing

Gramps Goes to College

In Gramps' Shoes

The Unexpected Bar Mitzvah

http://donaldjamesparker.com

Movies from Rossetti Productions

Right to Believe

Where Was God

One More Round

http://rossettiProductions.com

Matthew 28:19-20
Therefore go and make disciples of all nations,
baptizing them in the name of the Father
and of the Son and of the Holy Spirit,
and teaching them to obey everything I have
commanded you. And surely I am with you always,
to the very end of the age.